HARDPRESS.NET
HOME OF HARD-TO-FIND BOOKS

Confessions of a School Master
by William Andrus Alcott

S

Pl

CONFESSIONS

OF A

SCHOOL MASTER.

ANDOVER:

PUBLISHED BY GOULD, NEWMAN AND SAXTON.

NEW YORK:

CORNER OF FULTON AND NASSAU STS.

1839.

Entered according to Act of Congress, in the year 1839,
BY WILLIAM A. ALCOTT,
In the Clerk's Office of the District Court of Massachusetts.

PREFACE.

THE following work is a faithful though pain[exhibition of facts as they occurred during ten twelve years of the life of a common school ma ter. It is called his " Confessions," because 1 errors, and confessions of error, appear to pr dominate ; especially during several of the fi years.

Some may doubt the utility of such an exhi tion of professional conduct and character, ev where the work is anonymous, and the real nam of all persons, places, etc. mentioned in it a carefully suppressed. They may say it is unca ed for.

But have they duly considered the wants of t common school teacher ? He commences 1 pedagogical career, of course, without any of t benefits of experience. Often, too, like the w ter of this book, he commences in ignorance. 1

CONFESSIONS

OF A

SCHOOL MASTER.

ANDOVER:

PUBLISHED BY GOULD, NEWMAN AND SAXTON.

NEW YORK:

CORNER OF FULTON AND NASSAU STS.

1839.

Entered according to Act of Congress, in the year 1839,
BY WILLIAM A. ALCOTT,
in the Clerk's Office of the District Court of Massachusetts.

PREFACE.

THE following work is a faithful though painf
exhibition of facts as they occurred during ten
twelve years of the life of a common school ma
ter. It is called his " Confessions," because h
errors, and confessions of error, appear to pr
dominate ; especially during several of the fir
years.

Some may doubt the utility of such an exhil
tion of professional conduct and character, eve
where the work is anonymous, and the real nam
of all persons, places, etc. mentioned in it a
carefully suppressed. They may say it is unca
ed for.

But have they duly considered the wants of tl
common school teacher ? He commences l
pedagogical career, of course, without any of tl
benefits of experience. Often, too, like the w:
ter of this book, he commences in ignorance. I

s compelled to learn almost everything as he advances; that is, by observation, experiment, and reflection. Is it of no use to him to have at hand, correct details of the experience and observation —the errors, the corrections, the improvements and the suggestions—of one who has already travelled the same road, " through good report and through evil ?"

To supply the want which teachers are apt to feel, in this predicament, is the main purpose of his work. It is intended, principally, for the teacher's own library. Nor is it merely a detail of common facts and common errors ; it abounds in principles—principles in their natural connection with facts, and as it were growing out of them. Every intelligent reader will perceive that as the writer rose by every fall, so he found new light and gathered new principles and new strength from every error.

This is one of the most obvious, as well as most imperious duties of life—to learn from our own errors. And, yet, obvious as it is, few duties— perhaps none—are more neglected. The example which this little volume affords, will, it is hoped,

stimulate not a few, of those whom it concerns
to this frequently neglected, but all important duty

But the work was not designed for teacher
alone.   It is intended, also, for school committees
school visitors, etc.   The author's experience a
a school visitor will afford instruction in matter
pertaining to that responsible office.   At the same
time, it is believed, that the familiar style in which
it is written, and the general novelty of its instruc
tions, should secure for it a favorable reception in
every family.   It speaks, in some instances a
least, with a loud voice to negligent parents.

a*

CONTENTS.

CHAPTER II.

MY FIRST YEAR.

SECT. 1.

FIRST DAY OF SCHOOL.

SECT. II.

GENERAL COURSE OF INSTRUCTION.

SECT. III.

PARTICULAR ERRORS.

SECT. IV.

RELIGIOUS EXERCISES.

CHAPTER III.
MY SECOND YEAR.
SECT. 1.
COURSE OF INSTRUCTION.

SECT. II.
SERIOUS MISTAKES.

CHAPTER IV.
MY THIRD YEAR.
SECT. 1.
COMPLAINT TO THE GRAND JURORS.

CHAPTER V.

FOURTH AND FIFTH YEARS.

SECT. I.

MODES OF PUNISHING.

SECT. II.

ATTENDING TO OTHER EMPLOYMENTS.

SECT. III.

LATE EVENING VISITS.

SECT. IV.

STUDIES AND METHODS.

CHAPTER VI.
MY SIXTH YEAR.
SECT. I.

SECT. II.

SECT. III.

SECT. IV.

1

CHAPTER VII.

MY SEVENTH YEAR.
SECT. I.

DIVIDED ATTENTION.

SECT. II.

TEACHING ON THE SABBATH.

CHAPTER VIII.

MY EIGHTH YEAR.
SECT. I.

GENERAL ACCOUNT OF MY SCHOOL.

SECT. II.

CAUSES OF FAILURE.

CHAPTER IX.

MY NINTH YEAR.

SECT. I.

A NOVEL ENTERPRISE.

SECT. II.

METHODS OF TEACHING. DISCIPLINE.

CHAPTER X.

MY EXPERIENCE AS A SCHOOL VISITOR.

SECT. 1.

EXAMINATION OF TEACHERS.

SECT. II.

SPECIAL VISITS TO SCHOOLS.

SECT. III.

MEETINGS FOR IMPROVEMENT.

SECT. IV.

INTRODUCTION OF A NEW READING BOOK.

———

CHAPTER XI.

MY TENTH YEAR IN SCHOOL.

SECT. I.

COMMENCEMENT OF SCHOOL.

SECT. II.

SPELLING, READING, WRITING, ETC.

SECT. III.

TEACHING GEOGRAPHY.

SECT. IX.

MY MORAL INFLUENCE.

SECT. X.

MY ILL HEALTH.

SECT. XI.

COUNTENANCING THE SPORTS OF MY PUPILS.

SECT. XII.

DISCIPLINE.

CONFESSIONS

OF A

SCHOOL MASTER.

CHAPTER I.

MY INTRODUCTION TO SCHOOL KEEPING.

SECT. I.

PREPARATION AND ENGAGEMENT.

My "Learning." Applied to as a Teacher. Difficulties. My Father's Management. The School Meeting. School Funds. Mental Agitation. Engagement to teach. Terms.

My preparation for school keeping consisted, principally, in attending the district school near my native home from three to four months every winter, from the age of four to thirteen, and a few months every summer from that of four to eight. It was, indeed, customary, in my native region, for boys to attend school, in summer, till they were about ten or twelve ; but my father becoming dissatisfied with the female teacher to whom I was

2

sent in my eighth year, took me out of school
and finding my assistance on the farm valuable, a
he had no other boy, I was not permitted to atter
any more, in the summer season. Between th
ages of thirteen and seventeen, I was permitter
however, to go to school to the parish ministe
who kept a kind of high school every winter, i
all about six months.

One or two of my first teachers succeeded i
inspiring me with emulation and ambition; an
being naturally of a sanguine temperament, wit
a retentive memory, I usually succeeded in attair
ing and keeping at the head of the class; even i
spite of the efforts of those who were much olde
than myself to " get above me," as it was calle
It was, of course, soon noised abroad that I wa
very " forward;" had " good learning," etc. Th
in truth only meant, had it been duly analyzer
that I was a good monkey or parrot; for prece
dence in the class was made to depend wholly o
our skill at the mere spelling of words—and tha
too, by rote, or column. But no matter for that
such was the common report; and I had all th
credit of it.

This reputation, and the ease I found of keepin
at the head of my class, without much study, lul
ed me into a kind of indolence in school, to whic
I was not naturally inclined. It is true that I mad

some progress in reading, and still more in writing ; yet my progress was nothing in comparison with what it should have been. Two summers and one winter had made me a " speller," as it was then called, and a tolerable reader of easy lessons ; and as arithmetic, grammar and geography were not tolerated, in the school, except sometimes a little arithmetic one evening in a week, my mind remained *almost* stationary from the age of five to that of thirteen. Still I had the reputation, as I have already observed, of possessing excellent learning.

I mention these things, not that I think them of much consequence, in themselves, but only because they have some bearing upon what followed, in my pedagogical career. For I scarcely ever had, in my early life, notwithstanding my ambition, one serious thought of " keeping school" myself. To a station so high, I had not at that time, the presumption to aspire. I was indeed anxious for the reformation and improvement of the youth around me ; and for this purpose made some efforts to get up juvenile libraries, induce people to read periodicals, etc.

When I was eighteen years of age, my father was appointed committee of the school district in which he resided. The question soon came up whom they should employ to teach their school the ensuing winter.* It is true, no district meeting had, as yet, been held ; but it was usual for the neighbors to talk the matter over beforehand, in order to prepare the way.

Certain individuals—I never knew who, and no matter—suggested to my father that it would be well for me to teach the school. Your son, said they, has good learning ; he lives near the school house, and could board at home ; and your business is such that he could pay his board by his labor.

My father, though much flattered, was rather surprised by this proposal. In the first place I suppose he did not think I was old enough, or my judgment mature enough to teach a school. Parents do not usually think their children as mature as they really are ; especially boys. But, in the second place, the proposal was wholly unexpected ; especially, as the idea of teaching in the district where an individual had been brought up was not very popular in that part of the country.

Are you really in earnest, said he, about my son's keeping the school ? They assured him they were. It seemed to him, he said, that I was too young. Besides, I am not sure, he added, that my son could get a certificate. By this my

* It was not customary to employ a male teacher, in the summer, in that vicinity.

father meant a written license from the Board of School Visitors, stating that I was qualified for teaching; for without such a document no district school could, in that State, be considered legal.

There was another inquiry, very prominent in my father's mind; which was, whether his son had the art of governing well. This art was, in that region, regarded as a peculiar gift of Heaven. The doctrine that any person of good natural parts and abilities can govern well, or if not able to do so at once, can, by observation, study, and experience, soon acquire a good degree of this necessary art, had not, as yet, been brought forward in that region; and had it been so, would have been deemed a strange innovation—not to say a dangerous heresy.

But another question still arose. What was likely to be the compensation? Other teachers, for the first season, had from seven to ten dollars a month, and their board; though it was customary to "board around" in the families. But as it would be desirable for me, should I teach at all, to board at home, what would be the price, and how long the term? But neither of these points could be ascertained till a meeting had been held.

Here a still more serious difficulty met my father's mind than all the rest. Would it do for him to employ his own son? What would people

2*

say of it ?   The result of his reflection was to refuse to act as the district committee for that year; and let the task devolve upon some other individual; and then, if that individual chose to call a meeting, and the district, in that meeting, should vote to employ his son, why very well.   Having come to this conclusion, he forthwith—for my father was not a man of many words—shaped his course accordingly; and the mantle of office was transferred to one of my uncles.

Some persons were not quite pleased with my father's movements, but they soon learned the motive; that it was from a kind of delicacy on the subject—though evidently a *diseased* delicacy—and they submitted with cheerfulness to the arrangement.

A meeting was now called, and the subject of employing me was agitated.   It was customary to warn school meetings, in that region, by posting a written notice, five days before hand, on the school house door.   In the present instance I was requested to write the notice.   It was done in rather a trembling hand, and the lines " ran up hill ;" but, even with this drawback, it was a better handwriting than was common in the district.

I forgot to say that the school meeting was opened with only two or three of the proprietors present, except my uncle.   These individuals were not without objections to the plan which had been agitated; but as soon as it was guessed that I would be willing to board myself, and yet teach at seven or eight dollars a month, they waived them, and decided to employ me.

Winter schools, in that part of the country, were usually continued about three or four months; though the length of the term was always to be determined by the price of the master. They had every year about the same amount of money from the public treasury; and that was usually exactly expended in paying the teachers of the summer and winter school. If the teacher was employed at a lower price, his services could be continued longer; but if he was paid *more*, the term must be shortened. Before the State had a public fund, they had been compelled to tax themselves, not only in regard to wood and board, but also to pay the teacher; but it had now become quite uncommon to lay a tax to pay a master. Indeed, few thought they could possibly afford it. Though far more able to pay the tax their fathers had paid twenty years before than *they* were, they *felt* far less so; and while their fathers, had raised, in this way, some thirty, forty, fifty or sixty dollars a year, they thought they could not endure a tax of five dollars.

But as I was going to say, my father, who was one of the "noble few" who attended the school

meeting, was deputed to step home—a little dis
tance from the school house—and consult with me
There I was, trembling, and my heart flutterin
the whole evening, till my father came in ; for th
idea of keeping school had never before fairly be
come a reality ; I regarded myself so unfit for i
But I now had reason to consider it as quite
tangible concern, for my father had come hom
to determine on the number of dollars and cent
which must be demanded a month. He aske
what I thought I ought to receive ? The con
clusion was that I ought to receive ten dollars i
month, if I furnished my own board. My fathe
returned, and apprized the meeting of the result.

They at length consented to come to my terms
only instead of continuing the school four months
as had been the more common course in the win
ter, it was concluded to set it up for only three
Thirty dollars would be about as much of the pub
lic money as they could spare for the winte
school.

There had indeed been other objections. Some
preferred boarding a master, even at the same
price, because, as they said, it rendered him bet
ter acquainted, or at least more familiarly so, witl
their children. " Mr. P." they observed, " thougl
an old teacher, had, last winter, only ten dollars a
month ; and yet he boarded himself. Mr. B. is

to have only eight this winter, and his board ; and Mr. H. only seven."

You will not fail to perceive, from the general tenor of the discussion and arguments, that the principal reason why they preferred boarding a teacher was to save a dollar or two a month of the money ;—or if you should have any remaining doubts, they may very probably be removed in the progress of my confessions, in subsequent chapters.

SECTION II.

THE EXAMINATION.

Search for the Board. Introduction to them. Examination in Orthography—in Spelling—in Arithmetic—in Writing—in Reading. Why other branches were omitted. Examination concluded. Certificate given. Long Lecture from the Parson. Errors of these Examinations.

The next thing for me to do, was to be examined by the Board of School Visitors. In some towns this Board held stated meetings for the examination of candidates—a course which ought always to be pursued—but in my native town it had never been done. When a person wished to

be examined, he was obliged to " hunt up" the
visitors, unless—as sometimes happened, espe
cially if the candidate was a lady—the district com
mittee happened to have politeness enough to at
tend to it.

How I collected the Board, I have forgotten
Not so the results of the meeting.   These are no
so easily effaced from my memory ; nor will they
be till the day of my death.

I must now introduce you to the members o
the Board.   The first man was the village parson
who by the way, had been, for a few months o
two or three winters, my school master.   He was
of course, favorably disposed before hand ; though
I cannot help observing that he knew just abou
nothing at all of the wants of common schools
especially of the qualifications of a common schoo
teacher.   He was much more familiar with certain
medical nostrums ; for he had contrived to effec
the singular union of medicine—or rather of medi
cal quackery—with preaching ; how much to the
advantage of his parishioners, I do not know
However, he was the village parson ; and wa
therefore *number one* of the committee.

The next in importance was the physician. H
knew less of common schools, if possible, than th
parson ; though in other respects a better membe
of the Board.   He too might be expected to b

lenient, as my father a few years before had paid him a heavy bill for carrying me through—I do not say *out of*—a long fit of sickness. At all events he was a cheerful sort of man, and though it was whispered that he was a little intemperate, at times, still he had many traits belonging to human nature which were excellent.

Next came as member of the Board a military officer. He had been as high as " a captain" and had sometimes been thought of as a major; at least he himself had sometimes thought of it. He had, moreover, been a school master some twenty years before; but I do not know whether he was ever much esteemed in his profession. He was now fast filling with misanthropy; and had not the parson and the doctor been favorably disposed, I should have trembled for the consequences of his influence. Indeed, as it was, I trembled ; but not so much as I might have done in worse circumstances.

Three members of the Board made " a quorum for the despatch of business ;" and Dr. Physic proposed that they should proceed forthwith to the examination of the candidate.

The parson was to commence. How many sounds has B ? was the first question. Though B is called a mute, and is one of the more difficult letters for the embarrassed or diffident person to enunciate, and though I. did not expect they would begin thus, yet I soon recollected what I had so often repeated at school ; and faintly articulated ; B has but one sound as in *bite*.

How many sounds has C ? The reply to this question was more ready than the former ; for having once broken the ice, and that successfully, all now seemed to go on very smoothly. I could have repeated the " Introduction to the Spelling Book," as it is called, in which they were then examining me, from beginning to end without a failure. There was, indeed, a little trouble, when questions were asked promiscuously, but such an event did not often occur.

I was also required to spell. In this exercise, as I have already observed, I was pretty correct. I could not only spell all the common words of the spelling book, but also recollect them if they were separated from their companions. And although I now dislike this method of teaching to spell, believing it to involve a great waste of valuable time yet it certainly made *me* a speller. I do not remember the time when there were more than hal a dozen words in common use which I spel wrong, even in writing.

But I was required to repeat the rules of com mon arithmetic, and to read and write. The rule of arithmetic, I had at my tongue's end, and believe I understood their import ; particular pains, in this respect, having been taken with me by an assistant of one of the ministers under whose care I had, for a short time, been previously placed.

As to writing, my hand was too unsteady, just at that time, to permit me to write well. As the committee, however, perceived my embarrassment, and as some of them were already acquainted with the character of my hand writing, I found no difficulty. I learned afterward that they made the requirement as a mere formality.

My deficiency in regard to reading was most obvious. I read too loud, and too fast ; as well as in a tone of voice altogether different from that of common conversation. This habit I had acquired, during my first years at school, in reading in books whose language I did not understand ; and to the meaning of which none of my teachers ever furnished me with a clue. Besides I did not articulate well.

This branch, however,—strange as it may appear to some—the Committee did not deem an important part of their examination. They had embraced the opinion,—very common in the world, as I have since found—that a teacher who cannot read well himself can teach others to read well. They seemed wholly to overlook the force

3

of example in this matter, and the fact that children learn to read chiefly by imitating others. I do not say that they learn to *pronounce the words when they see them in a book*, in this way; but I do not regard that as worthy of the name of reading.

It has already been observed that Grammar and Geography were not taught in the school which I had engaged to teach. And as they were not taught, the committee were not accustomed to examine the candidate in regard to them. They had adopted the fashionable idea that it is unnecessary for a teacher to understand any other branches except those which he teaches; forgetting that the sciences are a circle, and that in order to have a perfectly practical and correct view of one, it is really necessary to have a tolerable knowledge of them all. Indeed, such an idea, at that time—I wish it were not so, even now—would, in all probability, have excited ridicule.

There was one more reason, I confess, why they adopted such a principle of examination. Not one in three—probably not one in six—of the individuals who presented themselves for examination as candidates for the teaching of our schools in those days, knew anything of grammar or geography; and some were mere blockheads in arithmetic. Had those branches been required therefore, the districts would have been deprived of their teachers; and this would in the end, have raised a "hue and cry," against the committee.

Shall the teacher retire, said Dr. Physic, while we consult together? That is quite unnecessary said the parson. Captain, said he, you are the youngest, what do you say to giving the candidate a certificate? Aye, or Nay? Aye; said the Captain. Aye, said the Doctor, in his turn And I say aye, too, said the parson. So saying they wrote me a certificate.

Before we parted, however, the parson gave me a long lecture on the solemn responsibilities about to devolve upon me, in my new and untried station; that I was to consider myself not only responsible to my employers, but to the children themselves, as creatures destined to immortality; and above all, that I must consider myself responsible to God. His remarks were excellent; but I suppose they did me about as much good as they usually do young candidates, in the same circumstances; that is, none at all. They are misplaced. They should come in somewhere else; say at the first official visit of the Committee to the School.

Was this the whole of the examination? perhaps some inquisitive reader may ask. I have related the substance of it; not always the very words. Nor have I related all the minutiæ of the conversation. What I have told is truth; only

I have not been particular to give the whole truth in every instance.

" Was nothing then said to you about the management and discipline of a school ?"　Not a word, that I remember.　All the examinations I had ever been acquainted with at that time, seemed to be based on the opinion that if a person understood a science or thing himself, he could teach it well to others.　As to governing a school, I believe I have already mentioned that the erroneous opinion prevailed, that this was a " gift ;" or rather as some seemed to regard it, a matter of mere haphazard.

I recollect, to be sure, that during the parson's lecture to me at the close of the examination, he said no teacher ought to go into a school *without a plan ;* but as he gave no explanation of his meaning, and hastened rapidly along to other subjects, I did not fully understand what he intended.

It is passing strange to me, now, that the manners and morals, and even the health of a teacher, are not made subjects of examination, at these meetings.　But were the propriety of either or all these doubted, I should still be astonished that no pains is taken to ascertain the candidate's views of discipline—of praise and blame, punishment and reward, and motives to action.　Would he praise largely and promiscuously, or sparingly and discriminately ?　Would he resort often to punishment ; and if so, to what forms of it ?   Would he allow of emulation as a motive to action ; and if not, what would he substitute for it ?   These and a multitude more of inquiries, in the same spirit, ought to be made.

Nor is it less strange—because the truth of the position involved is exceedingly obvious—that no pains is ever taken, at these examinations, to find out whether the candidate has the art of teaching what he knows.   A man may understand " all knowledge and all mysteries," but if he cannot communicate that knowledge or those mysteries, is he a fit teacher of either ?

It is also exceedingly strange that no efforts are made to find out whether a teacher intends to make it a great and prominent object to form the moral character of his pupils ;—whether he means to inculcate on every proper occasion, the great truths of the Bible,—and whether he means to en- force them by a good and christian—I do not say sectarian—example.   And whether, in the direct inculcation of truth, he intends to seize on favora- ble moments for doing it ; or whether, on the con- trary, he means to go straight forward with his instructions, at all times, without reference at all to the pupil's feelings, or to the circumstances with which, at the time, he is surrounded.

Lastly ; Why are no pains taken to ascertain

3*

whether the candidate for the sacred office of teacher, is truly in love with teaching? This is the grand point, after all. If a person has but the love of teaching, every other qualification will come, in due time. This, to the teacher, is what Paul represents charity or love to be to the Christian; the all in all. Give me but this in full measure, and if the candidate has a large share of common sense, is in good health, and even if he have not yet taught school, is not above thirty years of age, I ask no more. He will not be a first rate teacher to day, or this year; but he will be so in due time.

SECTION III.

MY COGITATIONS.

Plan. Anxiety. Dreams. Perplexities. Forebodings. Quite a mistake. The time-piece. Work for evenings and leisure moments. Approach of December.

The long dreaded examination was now over, and I was left to my own reflections. I was forthwith to be a school master. The school was to begin the first Monday after Thanksgiving; and Thanksgiving was near at hand. What now

remained for me to do, in the way of preparation ?

The parson's suggestion that every school master must have a *plan*, still rung in my ears. Wha
could he have intended by it ? Did he mean, in
reference to modes of government alone, or did he
also refer to methods of instruction ? I was hal
tempted to go and ask him ; but pride kept me
back. I was afraid he would think it argued
an inferiority of understanding. Strange mistake
When will the young learn humility ? Should
such a period ever arrive, in the world's history
then indeed may youth hope to become wise.

But how should I conduct a school, in regard to
methods of instruction ? This was a prominen
question with me, and filled me with much anxiety, whether sleeping or waking. I do not remember that I had ever thought, at this time, much abou
the best methods and means of securing good order and discipline.

I have observed that I was full of anxiety, sleeping and waking. Sometimes in fact, I could no
sleep at all ; but was forced to lie awake nearly al
night. This was more and more the case, as the
time approached for opening my school. Some
times I dreamed that I was already seated in my
pedagogical chair, and wielding, with success, the
sceptre of authority. Oftener, however, I had
trouble in my dreams. Not so much from refrac

tory pupils, as from forgetfulness, or some unhappy mistake.

Necessity compelled me to review, from day to day, my school-life. How were the exercises in the schools I had formerly attended conducted? Strange to tell, I could not remember. Or what is stranger still, I had not observed them. Is it asked, what I had been doing all my life long, at school? Almost nothing. As I have already said, I had found it an easy task to keep at the head of my class in spelling, and as this distinction was nearly the sole test of merit and scholarship, I made little or no exertion to do anything else.

It was the season of vacation in our district schools generally,—I might say universally, so far as that region was concerned. Had it not been, so great was my anxiety to know the usual routine of a school, that I would have visited one for the sole purpose. I was sometimes astonished that an absence of only five years from the common school room should have so completely banished its system and regulations from my mind. Whereas, the truth is—as I have already observed,—I had never really known them. My mind had been on amusement, when I was not closely occupied; rather than in the way of making observations.

I suffered terribly in anticipation of the difficulties I should meet with in conducting the studies of my pupils; especially at night, when I had time for reflection. More than once I would have fallen back from my engagement; but this I could not very well do. The die was cast, and I mus go on, prepared or unprepared.

When I reflect on the effect of my engagemen to teach, or my daily manners, I can hardly forbear smiling. I used to meet, often, with those who were to become my pupils. Instead, however, o conversing with them, familiarly, on the subject of books and school, I stood aloof from them, preser ving a kind of reserve and even stiffness in my demeanor, for fear I should otherwise lose the dig nity of the school master. Quite a mistake; though I was neither the first nor the last to make it.

The thought struck me, one day; what shall I do for a time-piece? A watch, I had never carried in my life. But a clock, in a school room, nobody at that time, and in that region, had ever thought of

A watch must be obtained. My father tempted a miser in the neighborhood to part with an old fashioned English watch, which he had kept among his dollars for many years; and this was to serve for the time-piece. Indeed it answered, in the sequel, a very good purpose.

The school was to be opened on Monday the first day of December. Our fall work was nearly completed; and preparations were made for me

chanical employments during the winter, of such
a nature that when I could be spared a moment
from the school, either in the day time or in the
evening, I could have full employ. Not a thought
was entertained—either by me or the parents—of
my laboring for the pupils more than six hours a
day. This was all that custom had required. A
teacher who should have devoted other hours to
his pupils—in preparing their copies, pens, lessons etc.—would, for aught I know, have been
regarded as getting insane. He would, at least,
have been greatly stared at.

How narrow sighted—might I not say how selfish—these views are! And yet they certainly obtain to a very great extent. Hundreds never think
of a teacher as any other than a sort of idle being. He is in school six hours a day, they admit;
but what is that? He has nothing to do but to sit
there, in a warm room, and hear the pupils read,
set their copies, and mend their pens, etc!

But who is the teacher—where is he—that *sits*
very much in school? I know hundreds of teachers; and among the rest, some lazy ones, who
sit all they can. But a greater number scarcely
sit at all; and some, never. And even with those
who are disposed to sit and do nothing in school,
it is very hard work. Most of them, at length,
find it easier even for themselves, to work than to

sit still. Six hours a day, moreover, is not all the time spent. There is an hour before school, an hour at the intermission, and an hour at the close of the day, the greater part of which most teachers are obliged to devote to the school, in some form or other. It is impossible to escape it if they would; and—to the honor of human nature be i spoken—many of them, after all that is said agains them, would not escape it if they could.

Here then are nine hours devoted to the school instead of six, which alone make a large part of the day, in our northern latitude, in winter. Nor is this all. I have known many a teacher who spent twelve hours, at least, in twenty-four, in thinking or acting, for his school. What do people mean, then, by *only six hours*? But to return to my story.

Time, though it seem long, never in reality waits. December was approaching. Thanksgiving, with its festivities and follies was already past. Nothing, at last, but a single Sabbath intervened between the young plough-boy and the pedagogue.

CHAPTER II.

MY FIRST YEAR.

SECT. I.

FIRST DAY OF SCHOOL.

Opening the school. Trembling. Letting pupils take their own course the first day. A misfortune. First Class. Reading in the New Testament. Second Class. Troubles of writing. Dismission for noon. One o'clock. Change of plan. Code of laws established. Its effects. Progress of the afternoon. Troubles towards evening. Threats. My errors. Reflections. Four o'clock. Dismission for the day.

MONDAY morning at last came, and with it the long waited for hour of nine o'clock. I did not suffer the village bell to strike, however, before I had rapped loudly on the door-post, with a thick, heavy rule made for the purpose. The pupils ran in, as eagerly as I could wish, but not as silently. However, I only said—'Take your seats,' in a dictatorial voice and manner, as the little urchins ranged themselves around the blazing fire; for tyrannous December had already made his appearance.—Every boy obeyed me as implicitly as if I had been the captain of a well regulated man-of-war; and every one retreated from the fire-place as soon as the word of command had fairly escaped from my lips. This was encouraging; but still I trembled.

Trembled for what? you will perhaps ask. I cannot tell you. Possibly it was because I feared I should not teach well; though I believe it was more from the fear that others would not think I taught well; for I was at that period exceedingly dependent on the good opinion and approbation of those around me.

I had commenced my labors with a sort of confused opinion—borrowed from somebody, I know not whom,—that on entering a school to which one was a stranger, it was a wise plan to let the pupils take their own course, wholly unrestrained, the first day, in order to find out the true disposition and character of each pupil. So I tried the experiment, or rather attempted it; for I did not get through the forenoon, without being obliged to use the word of command, to prevent the desks and tables from being overturned. I believe I had no whip thus far. A ferule I indeed had, but did not use it. By the way, however, I had been so exceedingly unfortunate as to *announce* my intention of letting them take their own course for the first day, as soon, almost, as we had assembled in the school room; which doubtless added not a lit

4

le to my wo. Had I said nothing of this, I might have gone through half a day, perhaps, without altering my original purpose.

But I made nearly as great a failure in conducting the lessons of the forenoon, as I did in regard to discipline. I had attended this same district school several years before—but as we have already seen I had forgotten the usual methods of proceeding. And of the possibility of a pupil's acquiring knowledge without going through a particular routine of class exercises, such as had existed in the schools from time immemorial, I had not at that time, the least conception.

One thing I had not forgotten, which was to have the older pupils read in the New Testament, for the first exercise; and to let each pupil read exactly two verses at a time. When I got the class fairly under weigh with this exercise, the agitation of my nervous system began to subside, and all for a time went on 'swimmingly.'

Soon, however, a dozen or two of the little fellows wanted to go to the fire. So I suffered them to go; but the question arose in my own mind, how many should be permitted to stand around it at once? There again memory relieved me. The rule of ancient times had been; ' only four at a time—two in one corner, and two in the other.' There was indeed room for more; since the chim_ ney was one of those old fashioned piles which occupy almost a quarter of a whole house, and have a fire-place capable of receiving well nigh half a cord of wood. But custom had determined the number, and I sought refuge under its sanctions.

When the first class had read just half an hour by the watch, the orders ' No further,' were announced ; and forthwith followed a general ' obeisance.' Then came the second class ; then the third ; then the fourth — who read in spelling books ; then a class in words of two or three syllables ; and lastly came abecedarians. It was wonderful how one exercise suggested another, on the principle of ' associated ideas ;' for though I began in the morning quite ignorant how to proceed in the beaten track which had long prevailed with my predecessors, I succeeded in going through the forenoon with considerable exactness.

One thing—the writing,—troubled me most Every scholar in the first and second classes, had brought a writing book, and wished me to write him a copy, and make him a pen. But this, to me, was an arduous task. True, it would have been less so, had there been nothing else to attend to, while I was doing it. But to be writing copies mending pens, giving permission to go to the fire and go out of doors ; and to hear and answer and adjust all the complaints which came to my ears with half a dozen other things, was rather trying.

However, I got through with the forenoon; but no one ever saw the sun approach the meridian with greater joy than I did that day. In truth, the classes had all read 'twice through,' at ten minutes *before* twelve; but as I thought I must not dismiss them till exactly *twelve*, with a great deal of difficulty I retained them till that hour; and then released them.

At one, the sound of my heavy rule on the door post, was again heard; and again the boys and girls were seen scampering from all directions towards the school room. Wheezing, and in some instances, coughing, they again placed themselves in the seats which they had chosen in the morning; which, by the way, were, in general, the very seats they had occupied during the preceding season or term.

" The first class," said I, " will now take their 'American Preceptors.' " No sooner said than done; so far, I mean, as ' Preceptors' were to be had. The ' Preceptor' was next to the Testament, the more common reading book for the older classes, in that region; but it usually happened that there was a little more than half as many books as scholars. " The rest of you attend to your studies, now," said a stern voice of authority, and, for a time, apparent attention was given, and the reading of the first class went on very well.

However, this first class had not yet finished their ' half hour,' ere the school grew rather noisy again. Commanding—not *requesting*,—the class to stop reading, I now told the school, most distinctly and decidedly,—and I am afraid, with a little anger, that I had altered the purpose I had formed in the morning, of suffering them to go through the day as they pleased ; that I found so many of them were inclined to behave improperly, that it was necessary to stop where we were and have a code of rules laid down at once. So I immediately began to lay down rules and restrictions, and to annex penalties.

This, at first, seemed to produce a favorable change in the condition of the school, and I began to congratulate myself on my supposed wisdom and complete authority. I little knew, at that time the unhappy tendency of *taking children to be bad* especially on the first acquaintance. Nothing perhaps, is more pernicious, than for a stranger to enter a school room, and lay down absolute and apparently despotic laws for his pupils. They see at once that he has no respect for them, which diminishes their respect for themselves ; and though various motives may operate to keep them for a short time from any gross violations of law yet they will usually break out sooner or later into acts of crime or violence ; or if they do not the teacher should attribute it to other and better influences than his own exertions.

But to return to my school.   Matters went on pretty well during the greater part of the afternoon.   There was little asking to go to the fire though there was more begging to go out, to get drink, etc., than in the forenoon.   There was less of setting copies and mending pens ; but there was quite enough even of these.   There were several roguish boys who seemed determined to do every thing upon which a prohibition had not been laid and as I had not yet established the old rule, ' write only a page a day,' a number of pupils had written out their page in the forenoon, and wanted a second copy for the afternoon.   The demand was more easy, as well as the refusal more difficult, than if I had not attempted to lay down, too early, an universal code of laws for the school ; but had waited a time, and only formed them as the circumstances and passing events seemed to require.

Towards evening there was some noise and disturbance in the school.   I had made a rule against whispering.   I had told them that if it were necessary—indispensably so,—to speak to a neighbor, they must either speak aloud, or ask permission of me to speak in a whisper.   At first there was little of either; especially of loud talking; for this was a thing so novel, that they seldom dared to venture upon it. As to whispering, though they usually asked permission in the first instance, they were very apt to whisper the second time without it; as if the permit extended to several acts, when it was originally intended to extend to but one. Finally, however, violations of the rule became considerably frequent, and I threatened punishment.

These threats, when they were first uttered, had some effect. 'If you do not stop whispering, I'll punish you,' was rather terrifying. But as the *mode* of punishment was not specified, and some of the threats, even against the same individual, were not executed, their terror soon began to wear off. I had forbidden any play, too, in school, and annexed to the violation of this rule, the same general, but indefinite penalty; and the results were, consequently, about the same as in the case of whispering. The school grew more and more noisy, my brow contracted more and more, and the pupils, of course, saw more and more the trouble I was in.

I had made no sort of allowance for the increased noise and whispering and play, from the consideration that it was near the close of the day, that there had just been a long school vacation of more than two months, and that it would take several days to inure my little group to six hours of sitting still daily, on hard benches; some of them without backs. I made no allowance, I say, for all this. No, not in the least! I demanded not only the same unconditional submission, but the same exact and unexceptionable quiet, during the last as during the first hour of the afternoon. Indeed, the errors of the last hours were less tolerable than those of the first, for I was more fatigued and my nervous system had become more irritable.

At that time I had no more thought of looking into *myself* for the source of the difficulties I met with around me, than of looking into the world of the moon. If things did not seem to go well around me, the fault lay in others—never in myself; so I thought, at least. What did I say? mistake. I did not think any such thing. I did not think at all on this subject; for I had not been led into the habit of thinking.

Had books for teachers, like those of Hall Abbott, and others, existed in those days, I should most surely have met with the principle some where in them, that if matters do not go well with a teacher, he should first look within himself for the cause; and there he will very often find it And had I found such a principle, I should almost inevitably have applied it to my own case and circumstances; for I was by no means one of those unthinking men, whom you sometimes find even in the chair of the pedagogue. The fact was, I was yet a mere boy, scarcely passed eighteen; and until a few weeks previous, had never in my life thought seriously of becoming a school master.

But once more to my school-room. Four o'clock at last came—the hour for closing the school. My brow, which had been for some time 'knit in frowns,' now partially relaxed, and I assisted the smaller pupils in putting on their coats and making preparation to meet the severe cold; for, as I said before, it was December. In rendering this assistance, I assumed the air of love and kindness; yet I am not sure that there were not some who regarded the increased and momentary cheerfulness and kindness, as proceeding from quite another source;—the pleasure of getting rid of my charge. Nor am I quite sure they were mistaken, if they did. But be this as it might, the school closed for the day, the pupils were dismissed, and the teacher was left to himself and his own reflections.

SECTION II.

GENERAL COURSE OF INSTRUCTION.

Teaching the Alphabet. My mistakes. One discovery.
How many months it takes to learn the Alphabet.
Teaching Spelling. " Going up." Long lessons.
Innovations. Reading. My own example. Correc-
tions. Another innovation. Its advantages. The
power of habit.

Having given a brief account of my " first day,"
I now propose to go into a little more detail on certain points. And first, of the general methods
and general course of instruction adopted.—Reading and writing have been indeed just adverted
to, in the last section.

Among thirty-five or forty pupils, I had three or
four who came to learn the alphabet. These
were seated on the lower seats, usually near the
middle of the room, and, during the first hour and
a half of the day, were destitute of any employment. All they were permitted to do, was to ' sit
still,' ' fold up their arms,' ' avoid playing and
whispering,' and ' hear the rest.' Or as some one,
versed in these matters has put into the mouth
of a young abecedarian, say A, B, and sit on
a bench.

How much they were edified by hearing the exercises of the older pupils, I will not now undertake to determine. As for the other requirements, they were doubtless very well, could the little fellows have lived up to them. But in order to have the whole room warm, the heat was sometimes very great in the central part of it—I mean in the centre and front, where the younger pupils were usually placed,—and it required no small share of philosophy to sit perfectly still for an hour or more, under such circumstances.

When an hour and a half had been expended on the older pupils, it came in turn to hear the little ones. One at a time they were summoned to appear before me. What's that? said I, pointing to A;—not the small a, such as is usually seen, but the capital,—What's that? This the pupil usually happened to know something of; so after casting a side glance on the school, in order to discover how many eyes were upon him, he ventured, in a trembling voice, to falter its name. Pointing to B, I proceeded—What's that? B. What's that? C. What's that?

By this time he had reached a region of hooks and crooks, where he began to be in doubt. So I pronounced the letter for him, and he repeated it after me. Thus I went through with the column of capitals without any serious difficulty; af-

er which, my pupil having ended as he began,
with a regular obeisance, was permitted to take
his seat.

I had not learned, at this time, the importance
of *constantly employing* small children in school ;
and that to sit an hour and a half at a time with
nothing to do, was as painful to them as it would
have been to adults, and even more so.   I had not
earned that it was better to teach them first, that
a before we teach the older ones, and before they
have become fatigued and wretched in body and
mind, by a long season of confinement ; or rather,
of imprisonment.   I had not discovered—and how
should I have made the discovery ?——that it is best
to teach the small letters before the capitals ; to
each the pupils in classes, rather than singly, and
o present a very small number of the letters, instead of the whole twenty-six, at a single lesson.

Of course it will not be expected, I had made
the still higher discovery, that it greatly accele-
rates progress, in these cases, to give to each pupil,
at suitable times, a slate and pencil, and encourage him to write the letters at the same time he is
earning them.

One discovery, however, I had made, which
was, that something was gained by saying to the
pupil, when his ' turn ' came ; you *may* come
and read ; instead of using the imperative mood,

as had been done from time immemorial. I had even gone a step farther; and daring as the innovation was, had found it useful sometimes to *go to the pupil*, and teach him at his own seat, instead of sitting still in my chair of state, and requiring him to come like a culprit, half dead with timidity, and stand before his master.

Most of my abecedarians, 'learned their letters,' I believe, in the course of three months; but I hardly know how. I sometimes wonder that pupils, in such circumstances, ever become able to read at all. But so it is. In the progress of three or four months, or at most in six or eight—two terms,—they usually get into words of one syllable; sometimes farther. So that though they lose, by our ignorance of the true principles and methods of teaching, three fourths of their time at the least; yet this is not so bad as it would be to lose the whole of it.

In teaching spelling, my practice was as follows. On opening the school in the morning, I used to assign to each class, a spelling lesson, consisting always of such or such a table, or so many pages, or a certain number of columns; and require them to study them; that is, read them over in a low whisper, or mentally. Sometimes I was in the habit of tasking them; saying that they must study the lesson over a certain number of times—

perhaps ten, fifteen, or twenty. And, in a few instances, I used to encourage them to compete with each other, by ascertaining who could soonest study his lesson through a certain number of times.

On being called up to spell, the class were required to read or study the lesson aloud; pronouncing, distinctly, every letter and syllable. Each pupil read two words at a time. When through, I pronounced a word to each, beginning with the pupil at the head, and requiring him to spell it. If he spelled it correctly, I pronounced the next word to another pupil; if not, the second scholar—or the first who could do it,—spelled it, and ' went up,' that is, took the place of the first, at the head of the class. But I need not describe the system of ' going up,' for it is probably well known to nearly every individual in New England.

My lessons in spelling were usually long, and I pronounced the words very rapidly, and required each pupil to spell without much hesitation and with the utmost rapidity. The longer the lesson we could go over in the time allotted to the exercise, the more progress it seemed to me we had made. How often I have boasted that we spelled *more*, in *our* school, than in any other school in the town! All this, too, without much regard to the manner in which we had performed the task. It is true I was glad to have my pupils spell well; yet after all, I made *quality*, in this exercise, wholly secondary to *quantity*.

As in teaching the alphabet, however, so in teaching spelling, I made one or two innovations. Although I had hitherto proceeded in the beaten track of my predecessors, it occurred to me, one day, that it would be better to have my pupils read their spelling lessons aloud before they studied them, than to do it afterward; because, in this way, they would be more likely to study every word correctly. So that instead of reading a lesson after it had been studied, and when we were on the eve of spelling it, we used always to read it, at the close of the exercise next preceding.

This was quite an innovation, I assure, you, for those days, trifling as it may now seem to many of my readers, and though a thing which in itself will not be regarded as of very great consequence, it may lead thinking teachers to investigate their own methods, and endeavor to ascertain whether they may not, in many instances, still be defective; and whether they might not make, in every department of instruction, more or less of improvement. And though many seem to suppose that they have already reached the utmost extent of real improvement, and that all beyond is mere innovation, may not the time come when they will look back upon their present course, and regard it as comparatively childish and irrational, as I now do my first efforts ?

But I must proceed to reading. I have said, elsewhere, that in reading the New Testament, it was customary for each pupil to read, at once, two verses. The exercise was usually begun by myself. I named the chapter, and after ascertaining that every pupil had his place, read two verses ; then the scholar at the head read two ; then the next ; and so on. I was to make the corrections—if anything was wrong,—unless occupied in writing copies, or in some other way ; in which case, the head pupil supplied my place. But though I often laid down my book to write copies, or to correct an unruly pupil, I seldom failed to read my two verses when it came to my turn.

Thus we went on, till one hour was passed, when another class took their reading books, and the same scene, in substance, was acted over again. When we read in other books than the Testament, the course was the same, except that, instead of reading two verses, each read a single paragraph ; or, if the paragraphs were long, to a period only.

The corrections which were made, either by my self or the pupil at the head of the class, were by no means numerous. They were usually confined to the omission of whole words, or to wrong pronunciation, especially of proper names. It was very seldom, indeed, that special efforts were made in regard to distinctness of enunciation, correct pronunciation, proper inflection, tone, emphasis, cadence, accent, loudness of voice, etc. There was a confused idea in the mind of both teacher and pupil, that if about *so many pages or chapters were gone over*, the art of reading would be the necessary result. How such an effect was to be connected with such a cause, I probably knew as little, or nearly as little, as my pupils.

Still, even here, I had made an innovation upon the established mode. It was not customary, generally speaking, for teachers to read, regularly, with their pupils. It was, it is true, done occasionally, but seldom if ever was the practice adhered to rigidly. But with me, it was a rule not to be departed from. I was as much obliged to read my verses or paragraph, as they were theirs. More than this; they were all permitted—and not only permitted but required—to correct me, if wrong in any respect; although I did not allow them, unless they were at the head, to correct each other.

As was intended, this plan had a threefold good effect. 1. It taught the pupils the importance of more accuracy in their own reading. 2. It renlered the school—so far as this exercise was concerned—the more truly republican. 3. My manner of reading was of great importance to them, as an example. Children learn much, even in the art of reading, by imitation. I am of opinion that nearly all the advantage which my pupils derived from reading exercises, during the whole three months I was with them, was obtained in this way. I do not say that they might not have gained other advantages. I now think that though example, in reading, accomplishes much, the correct practice of the pupils themselves does more. We spent time enough and more than enough, in reading, during the first three months of my teaching, to have made all the pupils in my two oldest classes excellent readers, had we pursued such a plan as was well calculated to accomplish the object; or had we pursued such a plan, defective as it may be, as is now followed in some of our best schools.

Sometimes, even then, I had many misgivings. I saw that we were wrong; and saw, to some extent, in what the error consisted; and more than once, resolved on a gradual reformation. I say *gradual*, for the public sentiment would never have permitted more than this. But I did not keep my resolutions of doing even a little. The power of habit was so great, and the old path in which I had been accustomed to walk seemed so much plainer than the new one, that in spite of all my convictions of propriety, rationality, and duty, I continued to walk in it.

SECTION III.

PARTICULAR ERRORS.

My "Nervousness." Fretting and Scolding. Their effects. Maxim of Salzman. Two teachers needed in every school. Why. Learning from dreams. My leading difficulty. Leading errors. Close of the term.

IT was my custom to begin the daily exercises of the school with cheerfulness, good spirits, great courage, and no little enthusiasm. I was also punctual. Never perhaps, in a single instance, during the whole term—unless prevented by some extraordinary occurrence,—did I fail to open the school at the precise hour appointed, viz. nine o'clock. This known punctuality had no little influence on my scholars. Example is, in this respect, as well as every other, more powerful than precept.

I did not, indeed, secure the punctuality of *all*. There were some on whom precept and example were alike expended in vain; though I had reason for believing, that in a part of even these cases, the fault lay with the parents. There are parents who cannot—so they say,—have their children ready for either school or church in due season. The mornings are too short for them ; or the weather is too cold, or too hot, or too rainy. The truth is, they themselves are too indolent ; for if neither school nor church was opened until twelve o'clock, their children would still be tardy.

As I have already said, I began the school every morning with courage and enthusiasm. For a time all things usually went on well. When there were any little irregularities in the school, I could easily correct them. A look or a nod, or at least a gentle admonition was generally sufficient. Or if the offence was inadvertently repeated—and there is more of inadvertence and less of obstinacy in these cases than is usually admitted, —I had patience to repeat the look or nod. I have even repeated it, with perfect success, to the sixth, the eighth, or the tenth time. Nor can I recollect at this hour—though it had never occurred to me to make the observation then,—that the fault was repeated with more pertinacity the tenth time than the second ; nor with less pertinacity after a whipping than after a nod.

I know this is a heterodox doctrine with many teachers, and with some parents. Children, they say, will gradually grow hardened ; and if nothing comes but looks and nods, these last will soon cease to produce any effect. This is true, most unquestionably, where the case is one of obstinacy ; but when the fault is that of inadvertence, merely, the whole case is altered.

Towards noon my pupils usually became more restless and noisy ; and the increase of noise and restlessness was greater in my own imagination— as I am now fully convinced,—than it was in reality.. I had *a nervous system*, and was sometimes prone to irritability. While my body and mind were fresh and vigorous for action, my nerves were steady and quiet ; but in proportion as I became fatigued with my labors, my nerves were agitated ; and I could not well bear with the very faults which in the morning gave me little disturbance. How then could I endure the same faults, heightened in degree ! I did not endure them with as much patience as I should have done. I sometimes scolded and fretted ; and sometimes I went still farther. Glad, indeed, I often was, when twelve o'clock came, and with it the hour for dismission.

An intermission of one hour, together with my dinner, partly restored me, and the afternoon, like the morning, was usually begun very well. For one hour there was little that I found it difficult to endure. The second hour became less tolerable. But the third and last hour of the afternoon was comparatively a Bedlam. I was fatigued, and so were the scholars. I was nervous, and they were impatient. I was fretful, and they were roguish. I scolded them, and they were only the worse for it. Lastly, I punished them, and they only hated me for the punishment!

How valuable to me, at that period, would have been the sentiment of Salzman, so faithfully reiterated in the pages of the "Annals of Education;" that if things do not go well in school, the teacher must first look for the fault in himself! How valuable, even, would have been the monitions of a faithful friend, in the shape of an assistant! Pupils will not tell us what the matter is. They know, though they may not be able to express it in words. They dare not tell us. They have never been encouraged to do so.

On the contrary, they have been discouraged from it. We have taught them—not in so many words, but by our carriage towards them,—to stand at a distance, and to beware of finding imperfections in the master. A faithful assistant— especially if that assistant were the son, daughter, or companion of the teacher,—could scarcely fail to discover the source of trouble, and would hardly fail, it is hoped, to reveal it.

When will every school, even the most humble, be furnished with two teachers ?   It is the opinion of some—and I am half inclined to the same opinion,—that our beloved district schools, the pride and glory of New England, will never become what they ought to be, until every one of them is furnished with both a male and female teacher.

Let me add here, that there are many reasons why every school ought to have both a male and female teacher.   I will name two or three of them. 1. This is the indication of Providence in the arrangement of the *family* school.   2. The modifying influence of female character in the daily routine of a school, has always been found exceedingly salutary.   3. It is a matter of economy ; as there are a thousand things in every school for which a female is better fitted than a male, while *his time*, which is far more valuable, can, by her efforts, be saved and applied to other and far more important purposes.

To return from this digression.   It was always my good fortune—and usually that of all the pupils, —to live through the day.   But how glad was I to see the school-room empty !   How has my heart—and not my heart merely, but the whole frame which it actuates,—leaped for joy, on finding myself once more a free man !   If I ever get through this term, I have said half a hundred times, it is the last time you will catch me in a district school. I will sooner beg for a livelihood. Nay, more, I will sooner starve.

Finally, however, I went to work to contrive how to manage better the next day. I have sometimes seated myself in my chair, and revolved the subject in my mind for an hour together. At other times I have taken my hat—the far better course,—and walked forth into a purer and more healthful atmosphere. I have often lain awake nearly the whole night, meditating what to do. I have dreamed and waked, and dreamed again; and sometimes I have derived great benefit from my dreams. I have dreamed of punishing a culprit; and of afterwards finding that the punishment was ill timed, improper, or inefficient. I cannot help thinking that the lessons of some of my sleeping hours were nearly as salutary as those of my waking ones.

Why is it that mankind do not try to derive more benefit from their dreams? I knew a teacher who made it an important point to get his pupils to relate to him their dreams. He said it gave him a better knowledge of their character. He found often, by this means, what their master passion was; a secret, as every parent and teacher knows, of very great importance in the management of a child. At the time of which I have been speaking, however, this, was a subject upon which I had bestowed very little thought.

I had one difficulty to contend with, which is not common with teachers. Not only was I young, and a teacher in my own native district, but my pupils were—a large number of them,—my brothers, sisters, and cousins. As it was a district where much complaint had sometimes been made of teachers that they had their ' favorites,' or at least their favorite families, I was prepared to hear their complaints this season.

Nor was I disappointed. I believe most honestly, however, that my own anticipations of such a result were the very means of bringing it about; and I am not at all certain but I might have gone on safely had I made no calculations of the kind. This *expecting* evil, is a great error ; and, in nine cases in ten, the parent or teacher who expects ill conduct in his children or pupils, will find it.

I confess myself not a little at a loss how to explain this phenomenon fully. I know, indeed, that if we *take* a family or a school to be badly disposed, they are quick to discern our want of confidence in them ; and, whenever this discovery is made, it leads directly to a want of confidence in themselves, and to a want of proper self-respect. But how it is that they can read our thoughts and feelings so readily, in our countenances and in our actions, it is not so easy for me to explain.

There was one point, into which my dread of evil made me run, which did much mischief. In the fear that the pupils would think I punished my own relatives more lightly than I did others for similar faults, I was apt to incline the other way, and actually punish them—especially my own brothers and sisters,—with more severity than others. This was all wrong. Children know what injustice is, much better than we are accustomed to suppose. I should have gone straight forward. Even handed justice is the best, in the end.

But three months—the term for which I had engaged,—soon passed away; nor was I sorry when it came to a close. We had *read through* the Testament, the American Preceptor and the reading lessons of Webster's Spelling Book. We had spelled all the columns of the tables in the latter. The pupils of the older classes, had *committed to memory* the ' abbreviations,' the ' pauses,' and the Introduction to the spelling book. Those who wrote, had gone through with a certain number of sheets of ' coarse hand' and ' fine hand.' Arithmetic, grammar and geography as I have elsewhere said, were not permitted in the school, at that time ; and perhaps it was well, all things considered, that they were not. The School Visitors had twice looked upon us, guessed a little what we were doing, and said all was very well; and this was sufficient. Every body then knew that they had a good school. I bought a few ' picture books,' one for each pupil, and distributed them, and read a long farewell essay—as was the custom—and the term closed.

SECTION IV.

RELIGIOUS EXERCISES.

Prayer—how conducted. Catechism. Effects of these exercises. My own example. My temper. Act of violence. Joining in the sports of our pupils. Unseasonable hours. Abuses and excesses. Sheltering themselves under the teacher's example. One cause of skepticism.

One thing in the first day's exercises of my school I forgot to mention, which was, that I began and closed the day with prayer. Not that I understood, at the time, the real importance of prayer in school; but I had a kind of confused idea, that all schools should be surrounded by a moral and religious influence; and I knew of no way to accomplish such an object but by prayer, and catechizing, and occasional lecturing; or at least I thought that nothing effectual could be done without their aid.

Since I have introduced, in this place, the subject of prayer, allow me to give you the results of my efforts in this department of my profession.

I knelt at my desk, and proceeded with great solemnity. Sometimes I extemporized; at others, I used selections from those excellent forms of prayer to be found in the Liturgy of the Episcopal Church. As the exercise was usually short, I found no great trouble from that want of attention, and that disposition to play tricks during devotional hours, which is not very uncommon; but had the exercises been as long as they sometimes are, in our schools, I think the case would have been far otherwise.

The duty of prayer was formally continued to the end of the term. The old custom of catechizing on Saturday was adhered to. I was also much inclined to giving advice, especially at the hour in which, above all others, it should have been omitted; I mean at the very close of the day, when the children were ready to start for their homes. How it is that teachers can expect to do their pupils any good by seizing on an opportunity for giving wise counsel and moral advice, when they are fatigued in body and mind, and are all on tiptoe to be dismissed, is more than I can now understand. But so it is. Many, like myself, fall into this error, and I find that not a small number adhere to it to the present hour.

'No good results ever followed, so far as I could perceive, from my efforts. They rendered the pupils no better disposed towards me, towards their parents, or towards each other. They still sometimes loitered on the way to school ; were noisy, uncivil, and unmannerly ; and sometimes passionate and revengeful. In short, they were just like other children in other schools, even in those where religious exercises were omitted.

I do not undertake to say that their errors, etc., were the *results* of my efforts. All I mean to 'confess,' is, that my efforts, even after they had been continued for months, appeared to make no effective impression. The children remained essentially the same. They were still, at times, selfish ; they still failed in self-government.

They remained, I have said, essentially the same. But I do not mean so much as this. Their minds and hearts became evidently steeled against religious impressions. They gradually came to regard prayer, and religious exercises in general, and even religious truth as mere formalities, or as an every day routine which must be endured, but which they would gladly have dispensed with.

How much they were confirmed in conclusions like these by my own example, I am wholly unable to conjecture ; but I tremble, to this hour, when my mind goes back to those early days and youth-

6*

ful scenes. It is true I did not swear, nor lie, nor gamble, nor drink spirits. Nay, I did not even smoke, or chew tobacco, or take snuff. I did not break the Sabbath—I mean outwardly. My conduct, throughout, was as good, externally, as that of many other persons by whom both I and my pupils were surrounded.

Where, then, lay the difficulty with my example? I will tell you. It was in the want of a truly christian spirit. Every pupil, in a school, knows—even before he can make the statement in so many words,—that the teacher, who professes to have a father in heaven, and to pray to him in school twice a day, and who catechizes his pupils once a week, and gives half a dozen, or a dozen moral lectures during the same time, ought to do something more than merely to refrain from open and flagrant breaches of the laws of the land, or even from the grosser violations of the laws and rule of temperance in meats and drinks.

When a pupil sees his master on his knees at nine o'clock in the morning, using the words of prayer to God, and then at half past nine finds him getting into a rage with Thomas because he is obstinate; or with Stanley because he is lazy or indolent; or breaking a large wooden rule across the head of Stillman; or striking Peter violently over head and eyes with a whip,—what inferences

will he not—nay, what inferences must he no
make? None other surely, than that such teacher
does not possess—let his profession be what it may
—that spirit of Christ for which he had just prayed
so long and so earnestly, and which, with so much
pathos, he enjoined on the school but the previous
evening.

Not that the teacher is set down as a hypocrite
or a jesuit, for one offence of the kind. Very far
from that. Children are by no means implacable
or wholly unforgiving; and if they do not forgive
quite to the four hundred and ninetieth time
they do not always give up a parent or teacher
otherwise excellent, merely because he gives ven
to his wrath improperly, in a single instance; nor
because he is irritable or unreasonable for a single
day only.

But when this is seen to be the constant tenor o
his life—when the child comes to the conclusion tha
the teacher's prayers have no habitual influence
on his conduct during the hours between—when
he comes, no matter how prematurely, to imbibe
a fixed opinion in regard to him, which is unfa
vorable, and to believe that he wears his religiou
character only as a temporary cloak,—or rathe
as a means of enabling him the better, perhap
the easier, to keep the school in due subordination
then has the teacher done himself, and even the
religion which he has assumed, a very great, and

t is to be feared, an irreparable injury. Then
nay it be at once perceived by every careful ob-
server, that the influence of the teacher's example
lestroys, and worse than destroys, the influence of
all set prayers and formal religious lessons of instruction.

I will not say that in my daily conduct, in
school, I erred to the extent which is implied by
the foregoing remarks. I will not own—for it is
not true—that I was habitually irritable or passionate. But there were seasons when I did not govern myself, and my pupils knew it. I remember
seizing a boy one day—rogue indeed he was, but
then I ought to have kept my temper,— and
dragging him by his collar over a large writing-
desk, not only with great swiftness, but with downright violence. I remember, also, that I often
struck the tender brain-case of even small boys,
with rules and heavy books—sometimes without
and sometimes with the certain indications of anger.

But there were other points in which I failed in
setting a proper example. I held it as a first principle, that every teacher ought to make himself
familiar with his pupils, from the oldest to the
youngest; and that he ought to join them in their
sports, or at least show a disposition to do so.

I shall not stop here to quarrel with the principle, but only to confess that I carried it to an extent which proved very injurious. I joined them, not only in sports which were rational, but in those which were wholly irrational. I amused myself with them at unseasonable hours. I showed, by my conduct, that I set my heart more on these sports, than, as a disciple of Christ, I ought to have done.

I have spoken of unseasonable hours. It was customary for the young at that time, and in the part of the country where I resided, to hold frequent parties of amusement in the evening, which both sexes attended, and at which they often had music and dancing. These parties were frequently the scenes of much noisy mirth and disorder ; and of coarse, and even obscene conversation,—to say nothing of other vicious conduct. Ardent spirits were sometimes drank in some form or another ; and it was not uncommon to witness cases of downright intemperance. Excess, both in eating and drinking, was very common. And these meetings were often protracted to an hour or two past midnight—sometimes till morning.

Now, reader—will you believe it ?—I frequently attended these parties, and if I did not go to the same excess with many others, I encouraged them by my example. This example I sometimes even heard them plead. ‘ The " school mas-

er " is here yet,' I have heard said more than
once, by those who otherwise would have gone
home and gone to sleep. I have had half my
school, or nearly so, present with me at one of
these wretched places, sheltering themselves under
my example. I have done these things, too,
within twenty-five years ; and within the very
heart of our own moral and devout New England !
Nor was I the only teacher who did this ; nor are
such teachers unknown even at this present hour !

With what face can such a teacher, after such a
night, meet his pupils at nine o'clock the next
morning, and invoke the presence, and blessing,
and assistance of Almighty God ? And how can
he hope to recommend to them, by example, that
religion which he is so perpetually trying to enforce by his precepts ?

I am not opposed to prayer in school, or to religious instruction. But I *am* opposed to a course
of management that is calculated to defeat the
very ends of prayer, and to disgust pupils with
every thing that pertains to religion. And when
I look at the daily walk and conversation of a multitude of teachers, who are, in the main, far better men than I was, and find them setting their
pupils a constant example of levity, or indolence,
or pride, or foppery, or slander, or deceit, or world-
ly-mindedness ; when I find them, in short, loving

the praise of man and of the world, except while in
their schools—perhaps even there,—more than
the praise of God, I cannot wonder that skepticism
exists among us; nor that some very good men,
discouraged by the abuses of a good thing, are becoming indifferent, if not averse, to the old ways,
and puritan land marks of our common schools—
those schools, which, with all their errors and defects, have been the most efficient means of
making New England what it always has been,
and still is, a nursery, whence are annually trans-
planted some of the most active men, both bad and
good, that the world has yet seen.

CHAPTER III.

MY SECOND YEAR.

SECT I.

COURSE OF INSTRUCTION.

invited to teach School again. Faculty of Governing.
Thoughts about getting a License. Examination.
Commencement of the School. Course of Instruc-
tion. Errors. Serious affair with George. Another
trouble. Am accused of partiality. " Barring out."
Caution to Teachers. Results of my Efforts.

My confessions, thus far, relate to the first three
months only, of my pedagogical career. I have
already said, that I was glad when the term expired. Indeed I was so; and it was my opinion,
at the time, that I should make no more attempts
at school-keeping.

But after another summer's work in the field,
and after the ' latter harvest ' was fairly gathered
in, I received an invitation to take charge of a
small school in a neighboring town for the ensuing
winter. I hesitated at first. I remembered, too
well, the torments and perplexities of the preceding winter, to be caught again without reflection.

But the price was rather tempting. Eleven dollars a month and my board, for a term of four months, were offered. This sum, which I well knew, by arithmetic, would amount to forty-four dollars, was quite a large sum for a boy of nineteen to receive for the labors of only sixteen weeks. I therefore concluded, at length, to engage and try my luck once more.

Try my *luck*, did I say ? Yes, I did ; for it was verily believed, in those days, that the art of managing a school—or even a family—was either a *faculty* or *gift*, born with us, or a matter of haphazard. This was especially true, in regard to the matter of governing. Few were expected to govern well, because few were supposed to be endowed—by the Creator—with the proper *gift*. And yet the question seemed, at that period, to have hardly agitated the human mind, at least in that particular region, why this same Creator should make us almost all teachers, either of families or schools, and yet withhold from all but a favored few, this most indispensable art of governing. But I have spoken of this at sufficient length in another place.

The principal thing remaining, in the work of preparation for my second winter, was to get a license from the Visitors. This was deemed by most young teachers as a great trial. But i

7

must be met. It was a war, from which there was no discharge. So, in process of time, I appeared before them to pass, if possible, the fiery ordeal.

Here, instead of the fiery trial I expected, I met a ' few good-natured fellows,' who just asked me to write my name, spell a few words, and read a paragraph or two in Webster's spelling-book. I said I read a paragraph or two; but this was hardly done; for I cannot say I was fairly through with my second paragraph before one of the company, who seemed to be the chairman, cracked a joke upon some of the sentiments it contained, and, turning to the table, wrote and gave me a license. The secret of all this, as I suppose, was, they heard I had taught school before, and that the school in which I was now engaged was small and in a remote part of the town; and any body, they thought, especially one who has ever taught before, can teach such a school.

But though my school was small, in point of numbers, it contained many large scholars—some almost as large as I was—and several who were older. These scholars were, however, much less advanced in knowledge and wisdom than they were in bodily size and strength.

The same general course was adopted, in regard to instruction, which I had pursued the previous winter. There was one thing, it is true, whicl made it somewhat difficult. The studies durin; the preceding winter, were spelling, reading an writing only. But a number of my older pupil: this winter wished to study arithmetic ; and some of them were desirous of devoting nearly thei: whole attention to it. As it was not very com mon in that region to admit arithmetic into the day school, I was not without fears that those who sen none but very young pupils would object to my devoting much of my time to this branch. How ever, no one objected, and all went on, for some time, very well.

Indeed, I doubt not I should have had a first-rati school, had it not been for two failures connected with discipline. For though I had something o the gift of governing well, as it was called, yet still adhered quite too much to occasional severity such as boxing the ears, throwing wooden rules and books, shaking with violence, etc. I believe I broke no rules on the heads of my pupils thi; winter ; but a circumstance occurred one day ¬vhich was scarcely less reprehensible.

George, with a young companion of his, was a play—for I had furnished them with very little employment of an interesting nature, and why should they not play ?—and my patience being nearly exhausted, I threw a rule at George witl such violence that, hitting him near one eye, it tore off a small piece of skin. You cannot conceive the anguish of my mind at the thought of hitting him in such a place, and of his narrow escape from the loss of an eye. I *knew*, almost before the piece of wood struck him, that it would be the last time I should throw a rule at a scholar; and such I believe it proved. I do not remember repeating the act from that day to this, and it is now twenty years since.

The father and mother of George reminded me of my imprudence, a few days afterward, but did not loudly complain. I believe they discovered that I was repentant; and of course, as judicious people, repentance and reformation was all they could ask.

Another trouble was more serious still. I have already mentioned that a number of my pupils were as old, and some older, than myself. This led me, gradually, to join them in their evening sports. Not that I had much relish for these sports, for I never had. I only attended them because I thought I must do so, in order to be respectable. Nor was this all. In the course of the winter I began to pay occasional visits to the family of one of my elder female pupils. These visits, though very unfrequent, gave rise to many remarks, and ultimately, to much uneasiness a-

mong my pupils. They believed me partial—
that I favored certain larger pupils, and neglected
others—and they gradually lost confidence in me.
Indeed such was the dissatisfaction, that as they
saw me coming one morning to school, they formed the resolution to shut me out of the school-room.
Their courage failed them, however, and the plan
was abandoned. This fact I learned, many years
afterwards, from one of my pupils.

I would here pause to request all young teachers to take warning by my errors. I have said,
on a former occasion, that I think it decidedly ad-
vantageous for a husband and wife to be engaged
as teachers in the same school; but for a young
man to be addressing one of his pupils is an unfortunate circumstance. In five instances in ten
it might lead to no difficulty; but in nine cases in
ten it might, and in a few it certainly would. It
is, at all events, attended with great risk, and
should by every prudent person, be avoided.

In spite, however, of all these discouraging circumstances, the school was regarded by many as
a good one. Perhaps it was so, comparatively.
Perhaps my pupils made as much progress, for a
time, as the pupils in neighboring schools; and as
much as they had been accustomed to do in this.
But this, though true, was not very high praise.
Something more belongs to a district school than

7*

the mere teaching of a little spelling, reading, writing and arithmetic. There are other sciences which ought to be taught. Then there is the teaching of example, and the formation of good and virtuous habits. These are as legitimately the business of the district school, as the inculcation of mere science ; and they conduce as much to usefulness, and much more to real happiness.

It was whispered, moreover, and from the results which followed, I believe it was generally understood, that I was a *smart* teacher ; by which was meant that I kept the school very quiet ; and this, in those days, was regarded by many, as the very summit of pedagogic excellence.

SECTION II.

SERIOUS MISTAKES.

Prolonging the afternoon exercises. Its evils. Shortening the intermission. Necessity of juvenile sports. Causes of a common error. My eyes gradually opened.

One serious mistake was made, this winter, which produced many unpleasant feelings among the inhabitants of the district, and which had I not been in other respects generally acceptable as a teacher, at least to the parents and masters of the pupils, might have destroyed much of my influence.

The hours for school were from nine to twelve in the forenoon, and from one to four in the afternoon. It was not uncommon for people to complain of teachers that they did not " keep their hours ," that is, did not teach the pupils the full *six hours* prescribed. Indeed I believe nothing was more common, with many of our teachers than to cut short the time a little.

This I despised. But in my zeal to oppose the practice, I went quite too far. There was indeed a temptation to this; arising from the fact that at this time I was strongly impressed with the idea that some how or other my services were valuable to the school, in proportion to the length of the lessons I gave the scholars in reading, spelling, etc. so that when I detained them, as I was apt to do after the hour of four o'clock, in the afternoon, or shortened the recess at noon, I considered it a real gain to the pupils, and a gratuity from me to the parents.

In winter, when in our climate the days are at the shortest, it is almost sunset at four o'clock ; and for little children, who have from one to two miles to go to reach their homes, the hour of four is quite

late enough to dismiss them.   And yet when the
weather was not too cold, I sometimes detained my
pupils till sunset.   I remember that in one instance
when they were kept till sunset, a fog suddenly
came on, and one family of children did not reach
home till dark.   No wonder the parents were
disaffected, and complained.   They ought to have
been disaffected.   They did wrong, however, in not
coming directly to me, and telling me their grievances.

This going and complaining to somebody else
—so common throughout society—is all wrong.
It is even unchristian.   " If thy brother trespass
against thee, go and tell him his fault between thee
and him alone."   The observance of this rule
would save much trouble in the world, and especially in schools.

But their complaints reached my ears, and I reformed my practice.   In doing so, however, I continued another error, which though it did not displease the parents directly, was very mortifying to
their children.   I encroached more and more upon
the intermission, sometimes continuing the school
till nearly half past twelve, instead of leaving off
precisely at twelve ; but always beginning again
precisely at one.

The first evil which arose from this practice,
was, that some of my pupils who went home to

dinner were not able to return seasonably for the afternoon ; at least they thought so. They had not time, they said, to eat their dinner. My reply to this was, that they usually had as much time for that purpose as I had ; for I boarded among the families and usually walked home to dinner.——I had not then learned that we ought to eat slowly. I supposed, up to this period, that the sooner we ate our meals, the better ; because the less we wasted of precious time.

Another evil was, that the pupils who remained, said they had not time enough for play. If the intermission was contracted to thirty minutes, and it took them fifteen minutes to eat, this left but fifteen for sports. However, I thought this was about enough. I had not learned, so fully as I have since done, that sports are as indispensable to the health of both the bodies and minds of children as their food, their drink, or their sleep. I regarded them as a mere waste of time, which it were far better to avoid. And with this view, the more I could cheat them out of their sportive hours, the better.

However great this error, and however common, I do not wonder at it, when I consider how ignorant people are of their own structure and the laws of their physical being ; and above all, when I consider how children are brought up. I was trained, as I suppose most others are, in New England, to the belief that play is folly rather than wisdom in the child; and that he will soonest be an adult who puts on the adult's gravity. In this belief, my father always gave me leave to join in the sports of my companions very grudgingly; and with the same mete wherewith he measured to me, I was disposed to measure again to my poor pupils.

My eyes, however, were gradually opened. I saw——how could I help it ?——that my pupils studied best when they had the most time for exercise. I found that besides a recess of ten minutes in the middle of the forenoon, and another in the afternoon, they needed at least an hour at noon; and it was accordingly allowed them. I gradually learned that their progress at school did not wholly correspond with the length of time during which they were confined to their seats, or compelled to hold their books; but that if they were cheerful and voluntary and spirited in their efforts, they might do more, in half an hour, than in a whole hour of languor, disgust or pain.

I say I learned all this; but, I repeat it, the knowledge I acquired was very gradual. I was always *slow* to learn from experience; though always making some progress. Alas, that young teachers, at this stage of their history, cannot be persuaded to study more the experience of other teachers by visits, conversation, and reading. They would then advance with threefold their present rapidity.

CHAPTER IV.

MY THIRD YEAR.

SECT. I.

COMPLAINT TO THE GRAND JURORS.

A " smart" master. Teacher's responsibility. Law making in schools. My own practice. Charles, his character. My adventure with him. He is punished. Col. K. His complaints. Unsuccessful. Interview with him. Acknowledgement. Reflections.

Early the next autumn, I was invited to take charge of a school, at a considerable distance from my former sphere of labor. What report, with her thousand tongues, had testified of me, I never knew ; I only learned that they wanted a " *smart* " *master*, and therefore came for me. The school, for several years had been taught in the winter, by easy, good natured, but rather inefficient men ; and they wished now, to employ a teacher of a different character. They wanted one who had the " gift " of governing.

They proposed to employ me four months, at twelve dollars a month and my board. I believe I have already told you it was customary in that region, with few exceptions, for teachers to go from house to house, and board in the families. I had done so, the previous winter.—The price offered me was so tempting, and the call so urgent, that I accepted it ; and my school commenced in November.

I had just now begun to feel my own ignorance, and to perceive the responsibilities of a school master. I will not say that I regarded these responsibilities as I ought to have done ; for I doubt, almost, if this were possible. Eternity alone, as it seems to me now, can set this matter in its true light.—But I felt them to such a degree as to give me much anxiety. How should I govern ? How should I begin ? How should I succeed ?—were questions that sometimes rested with great weight on my mind. I have lain awake a whole night, on opening my school, and sometimes nearly the whole of several succeeding ones, studying what to do, and how to manage.

One thing I had learned, during the two preceding winters ; which was not to lay down a code of rules or laws for my pupils before circumstances seemed to call for t'em. If you form your set of laws in the first place, it is as I have already said, but *taking the school to be bad*, which always has an unhappy tendency. It is the same thing, or at least has the same effect, as to express a want of

8

confidence in them, or a want of respect for their characters. And in proportion as they discover a want of respect for them, they will gradually lose respect for themselves. Now nothing is more deeply unfortunate to the young than a want of self respect. This lost, and all is lost. And anything which diminishes this is, I say again, of a most unhappy tendency.

My method was to appear to take it for granted that every one knew what was about right, and meant to govern himself accordingly. If he conducted improperly, I made strange of it, and gently reminded him that he had forgotten himself. This with most pupils—for indeed it was very nearly the truth—was sufficient. If however, a considerable number continued to disregard a certain thing, or to repeat too frequently, certain acts which I conceived were unfavorable to good order, and subversive of just principles, I then made a law against them.

Such a law, to be good for anything, must have a penalty annexed to it. This penalty was usually mild, but was always—unless it were in some very extraordinary case—inflicted. I had long before this found out that punishments, however severe, or however light, should be certain. Uncertainty defeats their whole purpose.

This may be the place too, for observing that I

had made some progress in the art of teaching. Not much, I confess—certainly less than I had in the art of governing or managing. Still I had done something. I had learned to pay my whole attention to a class while it was reading, unless indeed a monitor was, for a time, employed; in which case I sometimes ventured to be absent. But such monitors were very seldom employed; and in general, if I found it necessary to leave the class, I disbanded it. In short, I had come to a resolution to avoid, as much as I possibly could, the doing of more than one thing at a time. A most happy resolution for a school master. Would that it were oftener made, and still more often kept!

But the main object of my present article is to relate a curious incident that took place this winter, and which came very near breaking up the school, and destroying my rising reputation as a school master forever.

There was, in the school, a certain boy whom, for distinction's sake, I shall call Charles. He was always ready to play tricks when set a going by others; but he was not very artful in getting rid of the punishment due to a fault. Some children, you are aware, have the skill to do things which are wrong, and then shift the blame upon others. I had several of this description, at the time of which I am now speaking. They were even willing to unite in roguery, in order to enlist Charles; and generally skilful enough to escape censure, and involve Charles in trouble. Of this trait in their character, I was however, at first, utterly ignorant. Instead of regarding them as the ring-leaders—the seducers—and Charles as only an accomplice, I thought Charles was himself the ring-leader; and I at length began to watch and warn him. And according to the principles I have elsewhere advocated, the more he saw himself suspected, watched, and doubted, the worse he became.

At last, I began to threaten him with punishment. The results of these threats, any one who had a thorough knowledge of human nature might have foreseen. The boy grew worse and worse every day. The time finally arrived, when in my judgment, it became necessary to punish him.

Near the school-house was a large alder swamp. A boy was sent to this swamp to cut whips. I think his orders were to get and bring in three. The whips came. The boys looked affrighted. The scholars stared at each other, and at me. One young man of riper judgment than most of the pupils, hung his head. I now suppose that, knowing the character of Charles, he had doubts whether I was pursuing the right course.

The school room was rather small, as is the New England fashion; not more, I think, than fifteen or sixteen feet square. In order to make room for my operations, as well as to strike the boy and all the beholders with terror, I ordered all the inside, moveable benches, to be crowded as near the backside of the room as possible; took off my coat; directed Charles to rise, and begged the scholars to get as far as they could from the whip. Half frightened to death, the younger of them crowded into the corners of the room, while the larger ones, rather more fearless, sat and awaited the results.

Long and eloquently did I represent to the poor boy the nature and enormity of his transgression, and the justice of his punishment. His crime, I said, was obstinacy; and I thought it so. The boy evinced no deep sense of guilt, and I concluded at length to discontinue my speech, and commence with blows.

It happened that the rod which was used was rather dry. I made a parade of laying on very heavy blows, to put the school in awe. They were not so very heavy, however, after all. But the stick was so dry, it soon broke in pieces. One of its brittle parts flew against the cheek of a boy standing near the fire, and slightly broke the skin. —The delinquent was punished with some degree

8*

of severity, but there was nothing very remarkable about it.

After this was over, he seemed to behave better; as well as the whole school. There was not half the noise and disquiet and play that there had been, or else I imagined it so. In fact, I thought I could perceive the good influence of the chastisement for weeks, if not months afterwards.

However, about a month or six weeks—I have forgotten which—afterward, I heard a most singular story, abroad. Why I had not heard of it sooner, I cannot and could not then conceive; nor do I now recollect any better how it was divulged in the end. It was substantially as follows.

The master of the boy whose cheek had been wounded by the piece of whip, whom I will call Col. K. being very passionate, no sooner saw the cheek and heard the story, with all those exaggerations to which the boy's fright would be likely to lead him, was at once full of wrath and fury. He took his horse and sallied forth. To see me, do you ask? To see the committee? To see any of the rest of the pupils, to find whether their stories confirmed that which he had heard? No such thing.

He rode to the village and entered a complaint against me to the grand jurors of the town. He represented me as having abused—tyrannically and wickedly—a poor orphan boy,*—and as being wholly unfitted, by my ungovernable temper, for continuance in the school. He also told them how long the stripes were to be seen on Charles' back after the punishment.

It is rather to be wondered at that the grand jurors should take no notice of this complaint, strangers as they were to me. But such was the fact. The gentleman was not able to rouse them. Perhaps they saw what the state of his mind was —for he was so exceedingly angry that he appeared almost like an insane man—and concluded that the case was not *worth* their attention.

Here the matter ended, or would have ended, but for me. It is true that several persons in the district were dissatisfied with me, in a greater or less degree. But they knew better than to treat me in the manner Col. K. had done ; and between their sympathy for me and their indignation towards him, the whole matter was dropped.

For my own part, I was unwilling it should end thus ; I went to Col. K., and expressed, at once, a sense of the wrong he had done ; and concluded by asking him why he did not come to me

---

* Charles was, indeed, an orphan ; but this did not render discipline—provided it was the right sort of discipline, any the less necessary.

at once, as soon as he heard the story. Was it acting the christian part to go first to others?

"Sir," said he, "I did not go to you first, because I was not sure I could keep my temper. The children said you were in a violent passion and had whipped the poor fatherless boy almost to death; and I thought that if so, it was not worth while to go to you at all. Better go to the civil authority at once."

I asked him whether he still approved of such a course of proceeding; and as the stories of children, in cases of the kind, could not be wholly relied on, whether he did not think it better to go first to the teacher, and tell him his grievances—whether in short, if he were the teacher, he would not prefer to be thus dealt with. Indeed I pressed him very closely on the subject. It is true I did not fail to concede that there might have been something wrong in the course I had taken; but was this the way, I inquired, to set me right?

He frankly acknowledged, at length, that it was not. He said his only apology for the course he had taken was, that he was passionate. I was not sure, said he, that I should not *beat* you, if I met you alone, and while still enraged. But he now saw, he said, that he had done wrong, and was willing to say so publicly.

This was satisfactory; I could not ask more.

Though beginning to be conscious I had acted rather injudiciously, in some respects, and though Col. K. had not taken the best method of setting me right, I was quite willing to let the matter rest.

It is strange that while so many parents and masters are quite ready and willing to acknowledge that they ought to go directly to the teacher, if they suppose they have cause to be dissatisfied with him, and talk the matter over freely, so few will ever do it. They are more likely, nine cases in ten, to go to somebody else and complain. These things certainly ought not so to be! Parents! you who wish to have approved schools; remember that these things *must* not be so.

One word more in regard to my school. All went on well after this, for nearly the whole winter. There was no disturbance, no disobedience; all was quiet and orderly, as if nothing had happened. This use of the whip, on Charles, seemed to have accomplished its object completely. And though I cannot say I believe the rod ought to be much used, yet I consider, with Solomon, that to spare it entirely, in the progress of the education of our citizens, and above all, to proclaim that we will do so, is to spoil them. The rod is one of those things, which should always be ready for use, but seldom or never used; in the manner of physicians with some of their most poisonous medicines.

I knew one physician who carried a certain very active, i. e. poisonous medicine in his pocket about three years, yet with a firm resolution never to use it except in the last extremity. And though he had a tolerably large practice, as it is termed, he never did use it. And I verily believe that if teachers would make the same resolution respecting the rod, they would find fewer occasions, by far, for using it, than they now do. I know not why it is, exactly; but such is the fact—the expectation of a result always contributes to produce it. The man who expects to use the rod will almost inevitably be obliged to use it; while he who, without excluding it entirely, regards it like ergot, or prussic acid, or arsenic, or amputation, as a last resort, and intends to use it only when reduced to extremities, will find the demand for its use greatly diminished, if not wholly annihilated.

SECTION II.

INTRODUCTION OF A NEW SCHOOL BOOK.

Books in use. Danger of Innovation. An attempt. Successful. Character of the Book selected. Character of Reading Books for Schools generally. Singular trait in human nature.

For some time past, the only books which had been used in the school where I now was, as mere reading books, were the New Testament, the Columbian Orator, the English Reader, the reading lessons in Webster's Spelling Book, and Webster's Elements of Useful Knowledge. These had been read over and over; and every one at all acquainted with them knows, that except the Testament and spelling book, they are very poorly calculated to interest children, or instruct them in the art of reading, without special pains are taken at explanation and illustration.

I felt, most sensibly, the want of some new reading book for my school, this winter, especially for the older classes. But such was the universal fear of a little expense in the instruction of children, and so bitter were the usual complaints against a teacher who proposed a new school book, that it was almost as much as one's reputation was worth to attempt it. I however, at length ventured.

The plan was first proposed to the district committee. He did not object to it; thought a book was much needed; and said that he did not think many would be opposed to it. I rejoiced at my prospect of success, and already began to take courage.

But what book did I propose? he asked. I told him I had not decided on any; that there were many excellent books. He spoke with much

warmth, of the " Sequel to the English Reader."
There are some exceedingly *smart* pieces in that
book, said he, I should like to have it introduced.

In regard to the intrinsic merit and excellence of
the Selections in the Sequel, I had not the least
doubt. But I had some doubts whether it was exactly adapted to the wants of the school, and
whether it would interest them ; and I told him so.
He said we must endeavor to put such things—
books among the rest—into the hands of children
as we thought were best for them, whether they
liked them or not ; and that they themselves were
but very indifferent judges of what was really
best for them.

This, in the abstract, was sound reasoning ; and
I was quite unable as well as indisposed to meet
it. True the style of the " Sequel " was so elevated that my pupils could not always understand it ;
but then I thought we must *bring them up* to it.

The expense of the book was a serious objection, as it would cost as much as two books of
some kinds which might have been selected.
However, one good book was deemed better than
two poor ones ; and the Sequel would be a work
which it was thought would " stand by " for a
long time.

My present opinion that, other things being
equal, the two cheaper books would be far prefer-

able to the dearer one. I think novelty or change —some degree of it—is a very proper stimulant to the young. I would no more confine their lessons to the same book, than their bodies to the same dress, or their stomachs to the same dish. One distinguished teacher among us insists that every child who is pursuing a science, say geography or arithmetic, ought to study a great variety of authors. If this is so, it is much more true that a variety of reading books is indispensable.

But we decided on introducing the Sequel; and it was accordingly procured. In general it was favorably received. One wealthy widow-lady indeed complained that it was a "dreadfully dear book," and it appeared to her that something cheaper might have answered just as well. However, as the Teacher and the Committee both said it was a "smart" book, she would not complain; she would try to pay for it.

In fact it was much more favorably received, among the pupils themselves, than could have been anticipated. We are frequently gratified—as if it were an honor done to our understanding—when people present very wise things to our eyes or ears, taking it for granted we fully understand them. Thus we sometimes listen to a sermon or an oration with great pleasure, though we know

9

very little of its meaning. This is not said in justification, but in *palliation* of the measure.

During the first winter of my school keeping, there had been a similar occurrence. Some new school book was needed;—so I thought, and so did many others. The selection having been confided to me, I decided on the " Introduction to the American Orator." It was a learned work, prepared by a learned man, and wholly unexceptionable in its moral character and tendency. Still it was not at all fit for the pupils for whom it was procured, as time did not fail to show. It was only used a few years, when it gradually disappeared, and other and more popular books supplied its place.

SECTION III.

MEETING OF THE SCHOOLS.

Object of this meeting. My opposition. Dissatisfaction of my pupils. Greater dissatisfaction of the parents. Reasons for opposing it. Compelled at last to yield. The day arrives. Sufferings of the pupils. We mount the platform. Are reported the best school. Catching cold.

A custom had sometimes prevailed, in the town where I was, of bringing together all the schools at the close of the term, for public exhibition and examination. They usually assembled in one of the churches. The avowed object of the Visitors was, to excite public interest in behalf of Common Schools, as well as excite the pupils to increased effort. Whether the *real* object was not to save time to the Visitors, I never knew ; and if it were so, I could hardly blame them unless for their hypocrisy, unpaid as they were for their services.

Of the existence of such a custom, however, I had never heard, till towards the close of my school, when a gentleman observed, one day, that he understood there was shortly to be a meeting of the schools. I asked him what sort of a meeting ; upon which he stated as above. But the matter was soon settled by a public invitation from the proper authority.

To such a meeting, I was utterly opposed. First, from diffidence. Nothing embarrassed me more than to be concerned in anything which required speaking or acting before a large concourse of people. I had always kept open doors at my school room ; and had not only invited but urged people to visit me there ; but I was unwilling to submit to the drudgery or plan of going abroad to be exhibited.

Secondly, I denied its usefulness. The great object of these examinations—whether made at

ne school house or at the meeting house—is, or
hould be, to ascertain the progress and standing
f the pupils. The Visitors are supposed to have
already examined the schools, at least once, in the
arly part of the term, and now it is required to
now how much progress they have made. This
insisted could not be so well done abroad, as at
ome, in their own school room, and in their usual
laces and seats.

Thirdly, I regarded the practice as injurious
o health. The winter schools usually closed
bout the first of March, at the very worst season
or taking little children abroad two, three, four or
ive miles, and detaining them all day for public
xhibition ; especially as some are sure to be thin-
y clad.

For these reasons, I at first refused to attend,
with my school, and gave out that such was my
etermination. A few seemed glad of my refu-
al ; but generally it was not so. The scholars
hemselves, were, many of them, very far from
eing satisfied ; and the parents, most of them, were
more dissatisfied than their children. I believe
owever I could have carried my point with the
children, had the parents expressed no opinion.

They could not endure that other schools should
ttend, and not their own. Their school always had
tood high, they said ; and in more than one instance

had been at these public meetings, pronounced *the best.* And now, if I should not attend at all, they feared it would be regarded as a confession of inferiority.

With me, the last consideration would have weighed very little. I knew how much we had done, during the winter, and how much we had left undone. I knew that though my pupils were not all of them as brilliant as might be, their knowledge was in general substantial. There had been few set lessons for exhibition when visitors came ——common as the practice then was in schools. They usually read through the book, in course ; and if visitors were present, whether they were of the public Board, or, from private families——in short let them be whom they might——the sholars usually read the lesson assigned them at the close of a previous reading. And the same was true in general, of spelling lessons, etc.

I was therefore fully prepared to submit my school fearlessly to the examination——the thorough examination——of any body who might choose to look in upon us ; but I was not willing to go abroad, and exhibit ourselves to the public gaze But it was to no purpose to oppose the current The parents thought their children as good as those of other people ; and, like those of others, they mus be exhibited. So I consented at last to attend.

9*

When the appointed day arrived, no fourth of March was ever more tedious. I could stem the blast very well myself; and so could my older boys; but to take the little boys—and especially the little girls—and expose them to such severity of weather, was what I was utterly unwilling to do; could it have been avoided. But what help was there for it? Go we must, so, the weak minded parents had determined, if half of us were made sick by it.

To make it a thousand times worse, the church in which we were to assemble stood on one of those high bleak places which the first settlers of New England seemed wont to consider—like the Moabites of old—as more sacred than plains and valleys. Besides, the house itself was not more than half warmed.

A platform was erected in front of the pulpit, which the schools were required to ascend, one at a time, for performance. There were nine schools in the town, and each occupied the platform from half an hour to an hour, according to numbers and circumstances. Of course the exercises took up the greater part of the day. I cannot describe them minutely, it would require a volume; let me give, however, a specimen.

One gentleman whose influence had been considerable in " getting up " this foolish farce, and who, if I remember correctly, was at the same time both a committee man, and a teacher, had now on the platform, a fine opportunity to set off his talents. He was almost seventy years of age, had been much in the habit of teaching district schools, and thought he had attained well nigh to perfection in the art.—The day of wigs was gone by, but he came with his hair powdered, and as nearly arranged in the form of a wig as circumstances would admit, and with all the assurance and authority which belong to that ancient and venerable appendage.

In his exhibition of his school there was but one thing which indicated a wonderful degree of that wisdom which age and experience are apt to assume, whether or not they merit it. This was a reading exercise. He was in the daily habit in his school, of requiring a whole class of his pupils to read the same verse or paragraph together. His exercise has its advantages, but it is not the top stone of perfection in teaching, as this old man seemed to regard it.

He had selected for this purpose, and for this day, the seventh chapter of Revelation. All being ready and the signal being given, the exercise commenced. They were required to read slowly and distinctly; but in a key which was wholly unnatural, and with a force which was almost deafening.   The oddity of the exercise secured universal attention ; the attention of the old gentleman himself among the rest.   He was delighted with the silent tribute to the merits of the performance. His powdered wig was displayed exactly over the centre of gravity, and his giant form was as erect —heavenward—as he himself could have wished.   But when they came to read in a tone that must have awe struck every person not duly prepared for it, by previous notice, the words " Of— he — tribe—of—Juda—were—sealed—twelve— thousand," etc. the old gentleman was in an ecstasy ; and the audience were scarcely less gratified.   Had it been an English audience, the exercise would have been applauded by loud clapping, and I know not but the old gentleman would have actually arisen, like Mohammed's coffin, as far as the ceiling.   However, as it was, he did not ascend, but remained on the earth to teach by his example several years longer.   I believe, indeed, he never taught another school ; nor was it necessary, since he had brought the art of teaching so near the summit of perfection.

But our turn to exhibit at length came ; and with some twenty-five or thirty pupils I ascended (pale with cold and diffidence) the platform.   My school was not quite all present ; a few were absent.   If there was a timid or feeble boy or girl

who did not venture abroad, it was usually one o
my very best pupils ; and if I had a blockhead
who might as well have staid at home as not
he was sure of being present.

We got through, however, and for aught I coulc
learn, with much credit. Indeed it was very cur
rently reported, in our own district, that our schoo
was pronounced by the committee to be the
best ; and many believe to this day that such wa:
the fact.

There was one difficulty, however, in the way
of my believing the story. I found that the pa
rents and proprietors of the other schools had learn
ed too that theirs was the best ; and all from the
mouth of the same board of Visitors and examiners
—The truth was, that the board gave no opinion o:
merit, and made no comparisons ; such a course
not being their object. The opinions were eithei
uttered by somebody else, or were mere inferences.

But as I have already said, we got through ; and
nobody was ever more glad than I was, to have i
so. Many children took severe colds, but I do no
know that any of them lost their lives. The mis
chief actually done, in the way of laying a founda
tion for rheumatism, consumption, and fever, wai
unquestionably sufficient, in the aggregate, coule
it all have fallen upon a single individual, to have

lestroyed him; and perhaps to have destroyed
reveral of them. Yet as no one was killed out-
right, nobody complained, except, perhaps, myself. I preached long and loud against the cus-
om, and did all in my power to prevent the recur-
ence of a similar event; with how much success,
I do not know. I only know that though I taught
school in the same town several winters afterward,
I never heard of any more meetings of the
schools.

My school closed a few days after the meeting;
and we separated—for any thing we then knew—
forever.

CHAPTER V.

FOURTH AND FIFTH YEARS.

SECT. I.

MODES OF PUNISHING.

No whipping. Extreme silence. Procured at too muc
expense. One of the capital errors of my life. Bo
ing ears, and striking the head. Extent of this err
among parents and teachers. Attempts to correct i
We should " take time " for discipline. Reflection
on the use of the rod, and on corporal punishmen
generally. Consequences of blows on the head
and on the body. Further confessions of my ow
error. Regrets.

So well satisfied were the proprietors of th
school, which I had lately taught, that notwith
standing the complaint to the grand jurors, an
the opposition I made to the meetings of th
schools, I was the next fall unanimously invited t
take charge of their pupils again ; and I accepte
their proposals. In due time I repaired, onc
more, to the scene of my former labors ; and b
most of the pupils was received with a hearty wel
come.—I was invited to take the school the nex
following winter, but was obliged to refuse th

offer. I was however at liberty to accept a similar proposal the next year but one.

All went on these two winters—with few exceptions—very smoothly. I heard no complaint, about severity ; because I " whipped " nobody. I believe it was my boast, and the boast, too, of some of my pupils, that we had no rod in the school room, during the whole of the second winter. And yet it was commonly reported that such silence was preserved in the school that you might, at almost any time, have heard a pin drop.

I believe these reports were substantially correct ; and yet I can assure the reader I have very many doubts whether I governed the school *as well*, either of these two winters, as I did the first. I will present the reasons for this belief.

In the first place I think such unnatural silence, in a school of thirty pupils, is wholly unreasonable ; being procured at too great a sacrifice. There is not that freedom of action among the pupils which I deem indispensable to progress. I like to have a still school ; but I prefer a little of the hum of business to that stillness which is procured at the *expense* of business.

In the second place, the pupils did not appear to regard me as a parent so much as formerly. There was more of distance and reserve ; and less openness of conduct. The reasons of this will be seen presently.

Although, thirdly, I succeeded without using the rod, it cost an effort—and of a kind, too, which might have been very happily exchanged, even for the rod. I mean by this that in scrupulously avoiding what is called whipping, I reduced myself to the supposed necessity of using other modes of corporal punishment, which are far more injurious.

There is no error of my life—as a school master—upon which I look back with more pain than the one to which I am about to advert. Sometimes the reflections are attended with so much pain that I can hardly compose myself. Would to heaven it were possible to erase—as pencil marks from paper—some of the worst of our past errors. But no ; they are written with ink that is indelible. They are not merely printed, in the common way ; they are *stereotyped.*

What a sad mistake do parents and teachers make, who avoid the rod as with a kind of superstitious awe, and yet do not scruple to box the ears, strike the heads, shake violently, or beat or kick their children ! And yet hardly any thing is more common, than to shake a child with violence, or even to box his ears.

Parents or teachers who do this may rely upon

it that these blows upon the heads of little children are attended with far more danger than the blows usually inflicted by a rod of moderate size. It is not improbable that the intellectual faculties of children are sometimes seriously injured in this way ; and that some have been made idiots by it. Yet you cannot find one instance in a thousand, where any permanent injury is done by the rod, even where it is applied with a little too much severity.

Should these pages meet the eye of any parent, master, or teacher who is accustomed to make it his boast that he is not so vulgar, or old-fashioned, as to use the rod ; and yet does not hesitate to box the ears and otherwise beat or strike the tender brain-pan of his child, servant, or pupil, let him pause, ponder, and in the fear of God and of a judgment to come, beware.

I am not for encouraging the indiscriminate use of the rod. Nay, more ; I verily believe that in forty-nine cases in fifty of its use, it does more harm than good. But there are cases, occasionally, which in my own view, demand its use. They are cases, too, in which a judicious application of this instrument would be likely to accomplish the end in view better than anything else.

Let me say again, I am not for encouraging the indiscriminate use of the rod, either at home or at school. I go further. If parents and teachers were, from the very first, always truly wise, I entertain many doubts whether there would be any necessity for using it at all. Children would undoubtedly do wrong, but not maliciously or obstinately; and it is only in cases of malice or obstinacy, as I understand the matter, that corporal punishment is required. A moderate share of sound common sense—if parents and teachers would *take time*—would, in my view, prevent what it is often difficult to any person—but particularly so to those who are so unwise as not to *take time* for prevention—to cure or eradicate.

But neither parents nor teachers will take time to discipline their children in a proper manner. How often have I been pained, even in public discussions in " learned halls," to hear teachers of age and experience, and much supposed wisdom, gravely object to hearing even the details of those plans for managing children, which were designed to prevent the necessity of future punishment, solely on the ground that they would take up too much time. For what purpose is time made, if not to form and mould the character of those whom God has given us, and whom we profess to love!

But we live in a day when parents have too much to do to find time for bringing up their children. There are so many artificial wants of the body to be attended to, that the poor mind must shift for itself; or, rather must be left to starve. And as to manners and morals, these must be neglected and unheeded till vice is deep rooted and requires to be plucked up with violence. And lest the teacher should have any time to act upon the preventive plan, he is overburdened with pupils. The consequence is that nothing or almost nothing is done in the way of prevention; and the only alternative is correction or exposure to future suffering.

Now it is in precisely this case that the question of corporal punishment comes in. Here is a parent whose own errors have produced a necessity of correcting his child, in some painful manner. Shall the child go on to certain ruin, or shall the parent correct him?—you will say it is the parent that most deserves the correction; and I say so too. But will it answer the intended purpose to inflict the pain on himself? If so, every feeling parent, I think, would greatly prefer it. But it will not answer. The child must suffer, a part, at least; although it be for the fault of the parent.

The parent has erred. The teacher has erred. The child is beginning to suffer from the consequences. Those consequences are likely to run on through life—perhaps beyond it—unless the wrong, or error, which in the child produces them, is associated in his mind with suffering, or with the fear of it.

Now I maintain that the kind of suffering whicl shall be thus associated with the wrong or erro in the child, is not, in itself, of very much impor tance. Humanity would indeed dictate that i should be the least in amount which will answe the purpose ; but mere sympathy for the sufferer unregulated by reason, might sometimes lead u —and does sometimes lead us to prefer a mode which, though more easily endured at the presen time, permits a continuance of part of the evil and thus, in the aggregate, causes the child mor pain than some other mode which is, for a ver short time, more severe.

I do not defend the use of the rod, because the word rod happens to be found in the Bible ; for believe it is there used as a general name for al modes of the exercise of parental authority ane power. But I defend its use by parents and teach ers who are reduced to the dreadful alternative o inflicting pain, or see a child go on to suffering o to ruin. And I know of no method of inflictin; pain so excellent.

When you strike a child's head, even with the flat hand, you not only produce a concussion of the whole mass of the brain, but you endanger the hearing. When a child is pushed violently, o

:hrown down, or kicked, there is always a greater or less degree of exposure of the vital organs of :he body ; to say nothing of the danger to the eyes, :rom these random blows and pushes. Besides, you are very likely to stupify him, and thus produce insensibility to the smaller degree of pain you would otherwise inflict.

But when you take a rod of suitable size, and flagellate, even with some degree of severity, the skin, you may not only avoid all danger of injury :o any vital organ whatever ; but you run no risk of stupifying him. Indeed his sensibility increases rather than diminishes, as long as you coninue to inflict the blows.

The marks sometimes left on an obstinate boy, even for several days, do not necessarily indicate a degree of violence that borders at all upon inhunanity. Many a child has required a flagellation of this kind ; and would have been injured by any hing short of it. But how different is the comnon opinion ! "Such a little boy," I once heard a person gravely say to another, "should be vhipped little and often." Ah, it is these frequent mall whippings that ruin the young by thousands ! As a general rule, if we use the rod at all—remember I do not say a club, but a rod—it should e used with a good degree of severity : so that the smart may not only be considerable, but lon continued.

But it was far from being my original intentio to enter so deeply into this subject. I should n have done it, but with the hope of exposing th shameful and soul destroying fastidiousness abou the rod, which prevails with people who will n hesitate to box the ears and beat the head, an bruise the chest or abdomen; yes and 1 might sa produce more mental pain, and suffering than the save to the body.

To return to my own story. In avoiding th rod, I fell into the cruel and abominable practic of boxing the ears. In one instance I recollec that partly for an offence of some degree of mag nitude, and partly as a warning to the rest, I sai to a boy, " Now sir, as a punishment, I am deter mined to knock you down." So boxing his ear with a good deal of force, and at the same tim placing my foot in his way so that he could n step aside to preserve his centre of gravity, he fel over it. This boy, now a young man of almos thirty, always reminds me, when I meet him, o the circumstance; and says he thought, and stil thinks it a very unjustifiable sort of punishment and I think so too.——He used to say that if h lived to be strong enough, he would flog me, i return; but he has never yet done it. I hav been subjected however to a flogging much more severe—that of conscience.

I do not now recollect an individual whose hearing or whose faculties, any of them, were *known* to be injured by my blows upon his head, and yet *I do not know that it was not so.* I may have injured a dozen boys in this way; and the true source of their trouble may never have been traced out, or suspected.—As I have already intimated, though my fame was spread far and near, as a school master, this period of my career is one upon which I look back with more pain than upon almost any other; and could wish—were it not in vain—that it were blotted from the book of my memory.

SECTION II.

ATTENDING TO OTHER EMPLOYMENTS.

Evil results. How it interfered with my main employment. An anecdote. Caution to Teachers. Word of advice. Universal error among Teachers.

Some months before I commenced my fourth term in teaching, I had been made a civil officer, in my native town; and at the time I engaged to take the school, and even after I commenced, I had considerable unfinished business. This made it necessary for me to be absent from the school district, whenever I could, especially every other Saturday—our semi-monthly season of vacation. I was also absent many evenings. Nor did I confine myself to the finishing up of what business was before me, when my school commenced. New business came to my hands, and I had not the resolution to refuse it.

Do you ask why I should wish to refuse it, since it could be attended to at leisure hours without any interference with the school? I reply, that every teacher of a district school, if he does his duty and is thorough, requires many of his leisure hours, as they are called, for rest and recreation. The employment of teaching, whatever may be thought to the contrary, is not an easy employment. The teacher, if he is what he ought to be, cannot " sit there at his ease in a warm room, and get his ten dollars a month for it," as I have heard it gravely asserted. His task is exhausting, very much so ; and requires a strong constitution. And however strong that constitution is, it demands care and attention, or it will prematurely break down.

No teacher ought to have any other occupation, which requires much thought, or involves much

esponsibility.   He ought not, above all, to be a
ivil officer.   If he finds more leisure time than
s needed for exercise, and for associating with
he parents of his pupils, and his fellow teachers,
t were better that he should spend it in doing some-
hing for his school.   This would be true, if there
vere no interference of one class of employments
vith another.

But they do interfere.   Thoughts will rush in,
ncalled for.   More than once have the perplexi-
es of my civil engagements or duties distracted
ay mind, in the school room.   Nor was this all.
They sometimes led to the necessity of adjourn-
ig my school for a day or two.   This, though
are, did occasionally happen.

I have sometimes wondered how it came to
ass that the people of the district did not com-
lain.   But " the king," you know, " can do no
rong," and " he who gets his name up, may
e in bed all day."   I had acquired—though I
ty it myself, and though I have said it before—a
igh reputation in that neighborhood, as a school
acher; and therefore it was, perhaps, that a few
regularities did not easily injure me.

In one instance, I suffered severely from my at-
mpts to attend to other duties besides those of my
hool, and my pupils suffered still more than I did.
he nature of my office had led me not only to

be absent from the school one whole day, but to be up nearly all night; as well as exposed, much of the time, to the intense cold of one of the severest nights of January.

I well remember—for I can never forget it—what my feelings were when I went to my school the next day, after this night of suffering. The warm air of the room, joined to my need of repose, made me so sleepy that it was with exceeding great difficulty I could keep my eyes open. Joined to all this, my pupils seemed unusually noisy and troublesome; but the more I complained, the worse was their behavior; and it was with difficulty that I succeeded in getting through the day without resorting to the rod. I am now fully convinced that the fault was in myself; that the pupils were no worse than on any other occasion; but that the state of my nervous system after a day or two of great suffering and responsibility, and a night of fatigue and watching, was such as greatly to magnify the usual trials of a school room.

Let me here again admonish the teacher, not to have any other employment on his hands, while engaged in school keeping. No matter how low your wages; if you cannot live by your profession alone, abandon it at once; and betake yourself to some other occupation. I suffered not a little, during the first term of school keeping, by following a mechanical employment too closely, as soon as I was out of school.*   But this was as nothing at all to the evils of being engaged in the discharge of duties pertaining to a responsible civil office.

If a teacher wishes to become distinguished in his profession, he cannot be too exclusively or too arduously devoted to his school, provided he does not endanger his health.   He should cultivate a familiar acquaintance with the parents and masters of his pupils.   He should take great pains to promote the improvement of the children when out of the school-room, as well as while he is in it —their morals and their manners.   Let him not say; I earn my money, and more too, while in he school room, and I will employ my time in my own way out of it.   It may be true ; but you do not wisely to say it.   On the contrary, for every extra moment you devote to the duties of your profession, you may be richly repaid in preparation for the future.

And here I am reminded of one very common —I might say almost universal error.   Few teachers undertake the business of teaching as a means

---

* I think, indeed, that health in a school master requires that he should spend some little time, every day, in agriculture or gardening, or in some out-of-door mechanical employment ; but it should not be a business, but rather a mere pastime or recreation.

of procuring a livelihood, but only as a temporary concern ; or as a preparation for something else. As soon as business of a better character, that 'is, affording a better pecuniary compensation, presents, they at once abandon school keeping. On this account few take that pains to discharge their whole duty and to make all possible improvement in their profession, which they might otherwise be led to do.

But if they would consider a moment—and if to consideration they would add a little observation—they could not fail to perceive that every step of progress they make as teachers, is at the same time fitting them for future life, be their destiny what it may. The general rule is, that we shall be parents. And in what respect can a diligent teacher improve himself, that shall not, at the same time, better qualify him to discharge the duties of the parental office ? But should he never be a parent, yet he will find his every inch of progress, made in school keeping, of the utmost importance to him. You may observe a difference in this respect, even in the farmer or the mechanic. He who has been a diligent and persevering and improving school master a few years. will, other things being equal, prove a far better farmer or mechanic. To the truth of this remark I have never yet known a single exception.

11

SECTION III.

LATE EVENING VISITS.

'eachers ought not to keep late hours. Nor attend late suppers. My own practice. Sometimes misled. Visits among my female acquaintance. Importance of good company. Anecdote of a rakish school master. Night visits in general. Evening Schools. Caution to teachers. Example of Intemperance. Painful reflection.

There can be no objection to evening visits, rovided our stay is not protracted to an unseaonable hour. I have already advised teachers to ultivate a familiar acquaintance with the parents f their pupils ; and to this end it is almost indisensable that they should visit them during the ong winter evenings.

But it is not necessary, nor is it wisdom, to stay ut very late. They ought always to return to eir boarding place at nine o'clock. This is due to emselves in order to preserve their own reputaon in a world where slander has found its way nd is sometimes envenomed. It is also due to e school, before which he is bound to set a corect example in all things. It is, indeed, the only ourse a wise man will pursue, whether he regards nost his own health and reputation, or the welfare f his pupils.

I have alluded to one evil which results from late hours, or at least from long continued watching; and shown how it affects the nervous system. Late hours, in all cases, have the same tendency, even if they are attended by no circumstances which increase the mischief. We always become feverish in the evening, in a greater or less degree; and when we retire so late that the healthful state of the system is not fully restored, we are sure to suffer more or less as the consequence.

But when to late hours we add exciting drinks, or late suppers, or much noisy mirth, the evil is greatly increased. Even the old fashion of the country, of eating apples and drinking cider; or of " butternuts and cider;" or of using any other " eatable" or " drinkable," after the third meal has been received at the usual hour, is injurious; though perhaps rather more so to the school master than to the farmer; and this is the reason why I refer to it in this place. It is a temptation to which country school masters are very generally exposed

I was not much addicted to these errors; except to that of eating apples and drinking cider This practice was so common, in those days, and so seldom suspected to be injurious, that I did no hesitate to indulge in it whenever and wherever had an opportunity.

There was however another error into which

was led by the customs of the time, joined to inclination and that fondness which the young usually feel for something exciting. It was customary to form evening parties for the young, especially for dancing. To these parties the school master was invited and expected; and wo to him who did not obey the summons. He was considered as waning in complaisance to society, as well as deficient in spirit. As I had not moral courage enough to brave the odium which would attach to a withdrawal from these places, I sometimes attended. When I did, I was almost sure to stay late; and my school and myself to suffer from it.

But this was not all. He was not thought "up to the mark," who made not his evening visits, here or there, among his female acquaintance. The popular sentiment did not indeed require that any circumstances connected with these visits should be, in their own nature disreputable, or obviously immoral. But such is human nature that we do not always confine ourselves to the limits prescribed by public opinion; and I knew of some of my brother teachers who did not. And though my own conduct—for any thing I ever knew—was above direct reproach, yet I cannot but think such exposures highly improper. Is not a man known by the company he keeps? and if one school master in a town is an immoral man, by what rule are we to determine that the moral character of his associates is unexceptionable ?

One of the greatest rakes I ever knew—to call him by no worse a name—was a school master. He was abroad several evenings in the week, and frequently during the whole night. He did more, in one winter, to destroy the morals of the young, in the district where he was located, than a better man than he could have done to build them up in three. And yet nobody complained much. Had he not a right to do what he pleased with his time, out of school hours ? Happily, however, such instances are not very common in New England.

But all night visits, of the kind referred to, are exceedingly improper, as well as immoral; at least in their remoter tendency. I care not how guarded or qualified our approbation of them may be; it is all wrong. Christian moralists ought, with one voice, to proscribe all night visits in large crowds, however excellent the intention or object. A few neighbors intimately known to each other may meet with safety and even with utility provided they confine themselves to early hours, and to agreeable and improving conversation, and are without the accompaniment of eating, drinking, songs, or dances. These last should be confined to the hours of day, especially the afternoon. We want nothing after sunset to excite us; but

11*

every thing to compose and quiet us, in our bodies and in our spirits.   As a general rule, evening is the time for family enjoyment, and home is the appropriate place.

I am opposed to evening schools.   I used to indulge my pupils occasionally, in this respect ; but I would not do it again.   Six hours a day are quite enough for study.   I will not say that those who cannot find any other time to attend school, should, in every case, be denied the privilege of attending in the evening ; though I believe that even in these instances the person would often learn as much at home.   But the multiplied spelling schools and reading schools and " ciphering" schools of some of our country districts are a great evil ; and I am glad to find that judicious school masters are beginning to abandon them.

This is the place to caution teachers against mixing in bad company.   If there is a foolish old man in the district—or a young one—who knows no higher happiness than to hear jolly songs a whole evening, even though they come from the mouth of some drunken sailor, that man will surely, if in his power, entice the school master into the crowd.   But avoid such company, and such places, as you would the gateway to everlasting death !   The very same individual, mentioned in a former chapter, who attempted to destroy my reputation through the interference of the civil authority, sought with no less diligence—and came much nearer success—to destroy my character by introducing me to and identifying me with, such low company. I do not mean that he had any malicious intention ; I speak only of the probable effects of yielding to his solicitations. Thanks to Divine Providence, I escaped the danger.

I am more particular in dwelling on these small points, as some may be disposed to call them, because by all writers on the duties of teachers, so far as I am acquainted, they are overlooked. But there is one thing more ; and with that I will close this section.

One gentleman with whom I used to board several weeks of each winter used to bring around a quantity of brandy toddy every morning before breakfast, of which I was invited to taste ; and I used to accept the invitation. The man himself became a drunkard ; and it is said his only son— a scholar of mine at the time—is going the same way. Reader, can I ever know that my example did not settle the question in favor of that young man's present and future destruction ?

SECT IV.

STUDIES AND METHODS.

Methods in Spelling, Reading and Writing. Arithmetic. Writing down " sums." Reading Books. Reading with my Pupils. Not difficult to interest our Pupils in their Reading Lessons. Particular method in spelling. Errors in my course. Our reputation in spelling. Dialogues. Recitations in Grammar and Geography. An apology.

I have said that Arithmetic was not permitted in the school where I first taught. During my second and third winters, I had quite a large number of pupils in Arithmetic ; during my fourth and fifth terms, we had some Grammar and Geography.

Little however, was done, after all, except with reading, spelling and writing. The school was classed with reference to spelling and reading ; not so much according to real merit however, as according to age. The number of classes was about four or five. The first and second, or two oldest, were seated around the sides of the room. As the writing desks were placed against the wall, and most of these two classes wrote, they were seated here for the convenience of writing. When not engaged in writing, the desks served as a support for their backs. The smaller classes were seated on benches, without backs, in the interior of the room.

The school consisted of about thirty pupils. In reading, each class had four lessons a day; in spelling, two; in geography and grammar, one. The geography and grammar classes were however, small. The pupils were permitted to write and cipher at any time when they pleased; though the greater part of the writing was usually done at an early period of each half day. I wrote a copy for each pupil on one side of a quarter of a sheet of fools cap paper, and he was required to imitate the copy till he had written out the page; and only one page, in general, was permitted in a day.

In arithmetic each took his slate and pencil, and his " Daboll," and *worked out the sums* as well as he could. If there was a sum he could not *do*, and I was not engaged in something else, he usually came to me with it. The pupils would have gone to each other for assistance; but this I prohibited.

I had introduced among them the practice of writing down their sums in a large book. The object was chiefly to accustom them to keep memorandums, accounts, etc. in order, and with neatness. In this exercise some of them did very well ;

but others, unless constantly superintended, contracted more habits of slovenliness and disorder,
than of neatness or order.   I was never able, in
a large school, to control the practice so as to render it very useful.

The reading books in use, as we have already
seen, were the Sequel to the English Reader, the
American Preceptor, the Columbian Orator, the
New Testament and the Spelling book.   The
Testament was usually read by all the classes, in
the morning.   Each read, at a time, two verses.
In other books, each read either a whole para-
graph at a time, or to the first period.

I took great care to read, in my turn, with every
class, large or small ; and to read as well as possible.   I also frequently read the verse or paragraph which belonged to the pupil, requiring him
to imitate me.   Pupils in reading, I would again
say, are very powerfully influenced by example.
If I ever had any considerable success in teaching,
in this branch, it was the result of my constant
efforts to induce them to *imitate* me.

Near the close of the exercise, I frequently
read a verse or two, slowly, requiring them to tell
me the names of the pauses and marks which occurred, as fast as I came to them.   Sometimes
they " went up," as it was called, for this exercise,
as well as for spelling.

I had found long before this time, that it was not difficult to make children interested in their reading, even though the lessons were rather beyond their comprehension. This was done by conversing with them on the subjects of their reading, and make proper explanations. The only difficulty I met with in the prosecution of such a course, was the want of time. I could not, in practice, easily get rid of the notion that our progress in reading was in proportion to the length of the lesson—the quantity of ground—gone over; and hence we used to read so long in most cases, in order to finish a certain article, or such a number of pages, that it left us no time for any thing else.

In spelling, it was my custom to commence at the beginning of the book, with the words of one syllable; and to proceed through the volume, omitting usually none of the tables, from beginning to end. In a few instances, the larger classes went *twice through* in a season, but generally only once. A certain page, or number of pages or columns, was assigned each class, which they were required to commit entirely to memory. A few were found in the first class, who usually did this; but in general they fell very far short of it.

All the older classes were required to commit to memory several explanatory pages of the spelling book, embracing an analysis of the sounds of the letters, both vowels and consonants, with much other valuable information ; and also a table of abbreviations at the end of the volume, and an account of the pauses used in writing.   Every class, unless it were the very youngest in the school, was required to learn the abbreviations.   The smaller pupils often used to learn them by hearing the older ones repeat them.

At the close of every day when the spelling lesson was completed, the exercises were introduced of which I have just spoken.   They were merely recited ; no application was made to show their use.   Thus if a pupil who could repeat them from beginning to end, and knew how to say " *Messrs.* Gentlemen, Sirs" ; had found, in a book, or newspaper, " Messrs. Smith and Brett," it is doubtful whether he would have known the meaning.   Or if able to read it at all, he would probably say, " Gentlemen Sirs, Smith and Brett." And so of any of the rest of them.*

---

* 1 have known many an adult, who went through life with this ridiculous school boy error.   In like manner have I heard scores, if not hundreds of adults, who for the contraction *viz.* would repeat both the words for which it may stand, and say *to wit namely*.   They might as well or nearly as well, all their lives long, at the occurrence of *Rev.* at the beginning of a minister's name, dignify him with the double title of *Revelation*

Nor did my first class ever obtain many practical, valuable ideas in regard to the sounds of the letters. Thus, though they knew that *g* is said to be always hard before *a*, *o* and *u*, it is quite doubtful whether they could have applied the rule to the pronunciation of a word with which they were before unacquainted.——This, it is true, was not so much their fault, as mine. Had I taken time, it was perfectly easy to have taught them all this ; to have cultivated, in the exercise, their mental faculties, and powers of reasoning. It is not the study of mathematics alone that disciplines the mind. This result may be obtained in the pursuit of almost any science which can be named, if a right course is adopted——the course of reason and ingenuity and common sense.

In mere spelling, my greatest error consisted in requiring too long lessons, and in confining the pupils to the mere recital of the words in their order, in the columns. Had I taught them the use of words, in sentences, a shorter lesson would have done them infinitely more good than a long one without anything of the kind. To this end, I like very much the practice of spelling whole sentences. Thus a pupil may be required to spell ; " Water is transparent ;" " The sky is blue ;" etc.

Reverend. Thus he might say *Revelation Reverend* Mr. Smith ; *Revelation Reverend* Mr. Town, etc.

12

He may have spelled *blue*, in its connection with other words, a hundred times, and with correctness; and may even have told you the definition *color;* yet when you come to require him to spell the sentence, " The sky is blue," he may fail to spell it correctly; and if so, he would not be likely to *write* it correctly, should occasion require. Yet one principal use of the art of spelling, is, of course, to teach us how to spell well, when we write.

We had one exercise in school, which I am almost ashamed to name, which was that of speaking dialogues. It is true we did not take up a great deal of time with it; as the speaking was usually done out of school hours. Still it took up more or less time, and absorbed more or less of the pupils' attention, and ought not to have been encouraged.

In grammar and geography, the exercises consisted merely of recitation. There was no explanation at all. I would not give a straw to have a child of mine possess all the knowledge that the best of these pupils possessed when I left the school; with the exception of perhaps one girl. She seemed to understand, without explanation, whatever she put her hands to; thus confirming the frequent remark, that there is no general rule, without exceptions.

I have been thus particular in regard to these

exercises, not that the account possesses much of interest, but only to show the progress I made in subsequent years, in the art of teaching. It has always been my lot to learn by my own mistakes and errors; and if these mistakes and their subsequent corrections should prove instructive to others, the end of this volume will not be wholly unanswered.

CHAPTER VI.

MY SIXTH YEAR.

SECT. I.

TEACHING BY THE YEAR. TERMS AND OBJECT.

wenty-four years of age. What should I do? Keeping school for a livelihood. Offer myself. Am employed. Small compensation. Examination. Licenses.

Thus far I had only taught school for a term of ree or four months of each winter. In the sumer—as the custom was—my schools fell into e hands of female teachers, while I labored at me other employment, usually on the farm.

But I was now twenty-four years of age; and occupation was determined on for life. It was le to think of spending my time as I had done, vided among so many various employments. I ished to devote myself, for life, to keeping hool; but what encouragement had I to do so? ew districts employed male teachers, except in nter; and in those which did, I was entirely acquainted.

There was a district near the one in which I

had now been employed for three out of four winters, which was somewhat large and wealthy, although the people had never been accustomed to employ in the summer, any other than a female teacher. It occurred to me one day, that I might possibly take charge of that school for a year, if I would accept a very moderate compensation.

On conversing with one or two of my friends, who resided in the district, and stating with great frankness my object, they seemed gratified with the proposal, and promised to do what they could to have me employed. In regard to terms, however, they could not, they said, give much encouragement. I assured them that, for one year, the terms would not be a principal object. That I must be paid something, to be sure ; but as I was partially a stranger and they unaccustomed to the plan of hiring a male teacher in summer, I would accept of almost any compensation they might propose. Being urged, however, to name my terms, I fixed them at nine dollars a month, or 108 for the year and my board ; which last I was to receive, of course, in the families.

This was indeed a small compensation ; but I felt a strong desire to become a teacher permanently, and must begin somewhere ; and in order to secure this district, I was willing to make such terms as I thought would be accepted.

12*

A meeting. was accordingly held, at which it is decided to employ me for eleven calendar onths, with one month of vacation, at nine dol-s and board, a month ; which would be, for the ar, ninety-nine dollars. A friend, who had a rge family of children, offering to add another llar, and make up the sum to $100, I concluded accept it.

The circumstance excited some suprise through-t the town. What it could mean, for a strong, althy man, in his twenty-fifth year, to gage for a year, in a large school, at $100, ey could not conceive. There must, they ought, be some other object intended or aimed , or some deep-laid scheme to be effected.

But I was next to be examined for a license. r although I had already been three times exam-d in the same town, yet it made no difference. ie Board of Examination did not permit it to llow that because a person is qualified to teach school this year, he must necessarily be so for-er afterward. They only considered him qual-d, whom on examination, they found so.—I ve been detained by Boards of Examination, in mpany with a number of other candidates, till arly midnight, a number of times ; so long and lious were their examinations. Indeed, until I came quite an old teacher there, I was as regu-

SCHOOL MASTER.   **139**

larly and carefully examined as if I had been a total stranger. And I like the plan. It is just as it ought to be. I do not however like being examined at midnight.

But in the present instance—as formerly—I was licensed ; and I began at once to prepare for the discharge of my duties.

SECTION II.

DESCRIPTION OF THE SCHOOL AND SCHOOL HOUSE.

Former state of the school. Its size. Fifteen Abecedarians. The school-room. Location of the schoolhouse. No shade trees. The neighborhood. Schools regarded as a necessary evil. Immoral examples. Seats without backs. Sympathy and aid of the mothers. Beginning of operations. Effects of circumstances on the teacher.

The school had been, for several winters before I engaged in it, under the care of a very energetic teacher ; but the summer schools had not been so well managed. I had therefore a mixture of scholars—some bad and some good. The district embraced one street, rather central for business, and in which, as is usual in central places in our towns, there were a great many rough, ungoverned children; as well as a considerable number who had been injured in their habits, manners, and health, by over kindness.

The school was quite large. There were something like forty pupils who ought to have attended in the summer, and sixty or more in the winter. In addition to these, it was proposed to send a number from an adjoining district. I remonstrated against the latter proposal; but my remonstrances were of no avail. Two or three large boys—one as tall as his teacher—were soon sent in; and I had nothing to do but to make the best I could of it.

Among my pupils were fifteen little girls, who were yet " in the alphabet," eleven of whom scarcely knew a single letter; and some were but little more than three years of age. For me, it was quite a severe task, to take the care and instruction of so many very little children.

But my task would have been less severe had everything been well prepared in and about the school house. The school room itself was, indeed, sufficiently large, though the seats were not all good; but the arrangements of the entrance and out houses were far from being what they should have been.

The house itself stood in a real sand hill, on a road which was much travelled, which rendered it very dusty, in the summer. And a little way

from the school it was equally muddy and ur
pleasant. A worse spot for a school house coul
not have been selected anywhere in that regior
The only thing in favor of its location, was, that
was central. True, it was somewhat elevated, bu
not enough to answer much purpose in the way c
securing it from the irruption of showers of sand.

There was nothing like a shade tree, anywher
near the school house. The moment the pupil
were out of doors, they were exposed at once, t
the scorching blaze of the sun, if in hot weather
and to the full effect of the wintry blast in the op
posite season.

We were also surrounded by a neighborhoo
whose members were always suspicious of " schoc
children," ready to regard them as troublesome
and believe them mischievous. The truth is, the;
regarded the school as a common nuisance, an
regretted that they were obliged to live near it
and their only consolation in the case appeared t
be that somebody must live near it, and that pei
haps it might as well be themselves, as any bod;
else. How wonderfully philosophical the con
clusion !

It is a lamentable fact that people in genera;
in a majority of cases, seem to regard not onl;
school houses, but schools and teachers, as a sou
of necessary evil. They must exist, they know

but in so far as their mere feelings are concerned, they would very gladly have them out of the way. I speak now of common or district schools only. They cost them trouble and money.

Some indeed—a few—regard them as a convenience to themselves.   But the number of those whose first and deepest feelings in regard to them are attended with pleasure, and who view them as instrumentalities for the good of their children, appears to me exceedingly small.

The truth is, that the mass of our people do not consult the good of children in their management or bringing up, so much as their own good.   Children are regarded as mere instruments of their pleasure and convenience !   How small the number of those who regard, practically, the deepest import of the passage of Scripture which asserts that children ought not to lay up for parents, but parents for children !

We were not therefore situated unlike all other schools, in being surrounded by a neighborhood who were jealous of all our movements, and ever ready to attribute any little errors which might arise, to wrong motives.   Solomon says there is nothing new under the sun.—You see I admit the possibility of wrong being done by pupils to the neighbors of the school, for it is a fact too well known to be denied, that school-children are sometimes

troublesome ; enough so at least to feed that fir
of jealousy and suspicion which has an existenc
prior to the actual commission of any misdeeds.

One portion of the neighborhood in which w
were located was noted for dissolute morals. :
was a sort of rallying point for men of bad charac
ter. There was a mechanic's shop there, in whic
they were wont to collect at times, and exhib
such specimens of vice, especially of intempe
rance, as I was sorry to have my pupils witness.

However, in respect of society, we had not, o
the whole, much-cause of complaint. It was i
general excellent ; and with the exception jus
named, it was quite as good as usually falls to th
lot of a New England district school ; especiall
in a central position.

We had also many other conveniences. W
had a large, and for that period in the histor
of common schools, quite a commodious school
room ; It was well lighted, and could of course b
kept well ventilated. It was also susceptible o
being well warmed in the winter. There was
moreover, a larger and more convenient entrance
than is commonly found among us, for clothe
and other things ; and some very good writin
desks.

One thing was very soon discovered to be want
ing, which was, due supports for the back, to the

ats of the younger pupils. I had always felt
e want of these in my schools. But now, when
stead of some half a dozen little pupils from four
six years of age, I came to have fifteen abece-
irians, most of whom were scarcely four, and
hen I came to see them sit there on a naked
ece of plank for an hour together, I could not
frain from making a loud call on my committee
r some regard to their convenience. My call
as heard—not however without the favorable in-
rference of mothers—and backs were furnished
all the seats. This was the first instance of the
nd anywhere in that region, and probably one of
e first in the whole state.

We were now prepared to commence opera-
ons, and a commencement was made. I was
etermined to do my utmost for the school, not-
ithstanding the small compensation ; as my en-
igement was wholly voluntary. It is commonly
id that people labor according to their pay ; and
is a general truth. Here, however, 1 had other
otives to urge me on to exertion. I was begin-
ng to think of spending my days as a teacher.
y first object was therefore to teach a good school ;
y second, to have the reputation of it ; and a re-
ird to the compensation only occupied the third
ace in my mind. In these circumstances, and
ith these views, I was prepared to exert myself

to the utmost. Besides, the price, though low, was nearly what I had demanded.

I have mentioned with so much peculiarity, the motives by which I was actuated, during the year for which I was now engaged, in order that the difference may be clearly seen between the efforts of a teacher who feels that he is concerned in an employment which is to be his permanent employment—one in which and by which he is to gain his daily bread, and what is of more consequence, his reputation—and those of one who is only desirous of teaching a term or two as a preparation for something else, merely to busy himself till he can get a place which is more profitable. Could our common school teachers have before their eyes the hope of being permanently employed and adequately compensated, so that in this as well as in other professions or occupations they could sustain themselves and their families the change in the character of these schools would be very great. Never—and it requires not any special gift of prophecy to foretel it—never wil common schools be regarded as they ought to be till a man can sustain himself and family by thei united labor in and for the school.

SECTION III.

FIRST EFFORTS AT IMPROVEMENT. PUNCTUALITY.

My first object. Punctuality. My own example. Going without my dinner. Its effects. " Little things." Running to school. Apology. Telling stories to my pupils in the morning. Making fires and sweeping. My object in doing this. Why it is generally wrong. My devotion to my business. Results of three months' efforts. Regularity of attendance. A reform began, but not completed.

My first object, on opening the school, was to secure punctual and early attendance, in the morning. As in other schools, so it had been here, many were late at school, and some so very late as to lose the benefits of half the forenoon. This last was especially the case with those boys and girls—and there are usually several of the kind in every district school—who lived with masters rather than with parents; and whose masters were bound to send them to school a certain number of months every year. These pupils, if they were old enough to labor, were almost sure to be too late, both in the morning and at noon. The master or guardian seldom thought it necessary to send them till the clock *had struck* nine, after which there was some necessary preparation, and

perhaps a mile to walk, which frequently brough
the time of their arrival to half past nine, anc
sometimes to nearly ten o'clock.

I began the school by setting an example of
early attendance. I was always at the schoo
room before the appointed hour of commencing
the exercises; and when the hour arrived, I always began, whether I had fewer or more pupils.
No matter what the circumstances were; every
thing must yield, I thought, to punctuality.

In the long days of summer—and it was in May
that I commenced—I found no difficulty of getting
to school in season in the morning; though as I
boarded in the district and had often a mile or
more to walk, there would have been more difficulty in the winter. But in regard to the afternoon exercises, I had trouble.

There were one or two families, in the district,
who were gradually falling into the wretched fashion of late dinners. In one of these families it
was my lot to board for some-time. They knew
my desire for punctuality, as well as my fondness
for a good dinner; and that in order to have me
accommodated and gratified throughout, dinner
ought to be on the table at least half an hour before the time of commencing the afternoon session
of the school, viz. one o'clock.

And yet, with this knowledge before them, dinner was almost always late. I found myself under the necessity of eating too rapidly, as is the New England fashion, or of being late. One day when dinner came on at about eight or ten minutes before one, I took my hat, and without saying a word, went to my school.

There was no occasion, however, for doing it but once. The dinner, after this, came on early. It is true I gave some offence; but it was in a good cause. My point was gained, so far as this family was concerned. Nor did it end here. The matter was whispered abroad; and though some construed it into a whim of the master, or called him " very particular" about " little things," they all found out what it meant.

And indeed it was, in itself, a little thing. To have dinner a quarter of an hour later, for once or twice; to arrive at school late in a single instance; or to go without a dinner occasionally, was of itself, independent of any general principle or plan, which it affected, a matter of very little consequence indeed. But here was principle involved; and little things, where they involve principles of great importance, assume a very different aspect, and are, in reality, often among the great things of life.

My own punctuality, though slow in its operation, began at length to produce its intended effects. The parents seeing my determination—though they still thought I laid too much stress on small matters—at length began to yield, and make proper exertion to get off their children in due season. The pupils themselves, too, finding that the master was always on the spot before the time, were silently led to make more haste to be there in better season themselves.

Both parents and pupils were sometimes amused to see me *running* to the school, in order to avoid being late. They thought it very odd to see a school master run. He was expected to be a very grave, staid sort of personage, always moving—even to the tongue—both magisterially and mathematically. But they soon learned that there was at least one teacher who could move freely, and walk or run, at his option ; without fear of losing in dignity.

Fine confessions these ! some reader will, perhaps, by this time exclaim. What, does this writer mean to give us a long account of his own excellence, as a teacher, and call the work his " confessions ?"

Yet have a little patience with me, I beseech you. If there be a bright spot amid so much darkness and error as attended my devious, school master course, why not allow me to enjoy the pleasure of bringing it into view. My whole conduct, up to this period, or nearly the whole, appears to me, now, as a tissue of blunders. It gives me great pain to review it or to write it, and I would not do the latter but in the hope that it may be the means of helping on the good cause to which I then was and still am very much devoted.

Up to this period, I say, I had been greatly dissatisfied with myself, and with all my proceedings. During this year and the year following, though I have many blunders to confess ; I really made some progress, and produced some good impressions. Nor do I think it out of place to record them in this work.

But I have not yet told you all that I did to secure the early and punctual attendance of my young charge. I used to encourage them to come to the school room an hour, or at least half an hour, before opening the school in the morning, and hear me read or relate stories. A considerable number accordingly came, and I sometimes had quite a numerous class around me in the morning, hearing my stories. They were not only pleased with these exercises, but I verily think they often received quite as much benefit from them, at least morally, as they received from the whole subsequent exercises of the day.

They were not only invited to the school room thus early, but everything was made as agreeable as possible. With my own hands I made the fire as well as swept the room and arranged the seats I began to learn that a school room, to render children happy, ought to resemble, much more than is usual, the rooms to which they are accustomed at home ; and especially that it ought to be kept neat and clean.

I spoke of making fires, but it was in anticipation ; for the season of fires had not yet arrived When that season did arrive, however, I made the fires for the school, although such a thing was neither common, nor expected. It was usually done either by the older pupils, or by some neighbor appointed by the district for the purpose. But I found so much difficulty in having the work done well and seasonably, in every instance, that I resolved to do it myself.

It was the same difficulty that led me to sweep the school room. My female pupils were kind enough to offer their services ; but I thanked them, and told them I preferred to do the work myself. In this way I always knew what to depend on ; in the other way there was sometimes a failure. And nothing rendered me, in those days more irritable, than such an accident.

Here I was a little wrong. The thing intended that is, the comfort and happiness of my pupils was perfectly right. It was my duty to make great exertion, and even some sacrifice, to secure objects so important. But to do the work myself, and set aside the kind offers of the pupils, had at least two unhappy effects.

1. It implied a want of confidence in them, whereas it is one part of our duty as teachers to make them worthy of our confidence. But to make them thus worthy, we must confide in them. And although they should not do our work quite as well as we might do it ourselves, it is sometimes better to entrust them with it, and risk the consequences, than never to trust.

In this matter parents as well as teachers often mistake. The father and the mother will do things themselves, because their children, at their first efforts, will be awkward, or perhaps wasteful. But if the child is never put to a particular kind of labor because he cannot do it quite so well as the parent, pray when is he to learn it? Here is one great and serious error running through all ranks and classes of society.

2. No school master can *afford* to do these things himself. His time is too valuable. If he had not an abundant and even a superabundant supply of physical exercise without it, the case would be materially altered.* But he usually has.

---

* Even then, it would be better for him to exercise in the open air.

It were better, therefore, in general, to be subjec
to a little occasional inconvenience than to tak
the work out of the hands of the pupils and do i
himself.

I say it were better to do so *in general.* I sti
think there are cases where a contrary course *ma*
be properly pursued. When the whole distric
are asleep, as it were, such exertions on the pai
of a teacher may serve to awaken and arous
them. Such was the intention, and such was th
result, in the present instance. I do not think
was wrong in beginning in this manner; but I be
lieve it was wrong in me to continue it, summe
and winter, throughout the whole year. I cel
tainly should not do so again.

The truth is, I was wholly and entirely devote
to reforming the school. My whole mind an
heart and soul were upon it. My dreams were c
my school. I waked and rose early but to thin
of or do something for it. I conversed upon it,
possible, at breakfast; I hastened to the schoc
room as soon as breakfast was over; I staid ther
during the intermission, unless I was boarding ver
near by; and I remained at the school room afte
the close of the school in the afternoon, till dark
and sometimes returned, after supper, and spe
the evening there. In short I lived, during th
year, for no earthly object but my school.

I did, indeed, at the suggestion of a ministerial friend, undertake the study of a little Latin, but it was soon relinquished. I found it was enough—and more than enough—for one man, to take care of a large district school.

Three months had not elapsed from the time of my commencing the school, ere I had secured a good degree of punctuality of attendance. The pupils were nearly all present at nine, and at one o'clock. They were also punctual to the hour of class exercises. We had no clock in the school—a thing which ought to be furnished to every school room—but in place of it, I used a watch ; and as we had certain times for every class exercise, when a class was called upon, it was usually ready.

There was also greater regularity of attendance. Parents grew less and less fond of indulging their children in staying at home occasionally. Many of my pupils lost not a day, from one month to another. Irregularity of attendance, in most of our schools, is a sore evil. If people knew half the consequences, they would not surely be accessary to it.

In short, a reform was begun, externally. Had I known at that time, a little better how to carry the spirit of reform into the internal concerns of the school, much more might have been accomplished.   A good work was begun ; but it was not completed.

SECTION IV.

METHODS AND DISCIPLINE.

Methods of instruction. Spelling. Abbreviations. Pauses and analysis of Sounds. Reading. Reading Books. Writing. Grammar. Geography. Arithmetic. Book-keeping. My abecedarians. Discipline. Cases of corporal punishment. The Rod. Boxing ears. A Barbarous Occurrence. Subsequent regret.

In regard to methods of instruction I made very little improvement during this whole year. In spelling, I was still fond of putting forth all my strength, and requiring my pupils to do the same, to get long lessons ; still clinging to the idea, though I would not at the same time have defended it, in so many words, that excellence in spelling was evinced by the pupils in proportion to the number of words or columns of words they were able to repeat, by rote.

Were this a just test of excellence, our school ought certainly to have ranked very high.   For few schools, as I may safely venture to affirm—I suspect not any—could have been found, in which so many words were correctly spelled in the course of the day, as in mine. Yet had they been required to spell the same words promiscuously, or use them in composition, they would have made sad work indeed.

The pauses, abbreviations, analysis of sounds, key, etc., were however attended to in this school in a manner which was rather more intelligible than had ever been done in any school of mine before. I was in the habit—whenever I found time—of explaining and illustrating them, and showing their use by practical examples, much more than formerly.

In reading I fell into the habit, more and more, of reading every scholar's verse or paragraph, before calling on him to do it. I found it, as I then thought, of very great service. But I now think I carried the practice to an extreme which defeated, in a measure, my own intentions; for I sometimes tired the patience of my pupils, if I did not actually disgust them. So difficult is it to avoid having our favorites or hobbies, and riding them most unreasonably. The plan, with some pupils, and in some circumstances, is certainly a good one, and deserves to be imitated; but like almost all other good things, may be carried out to an extreme.

. Our reading books, as well as our other class

books, were much of the same general characte
with those which I had found in other schools
and such as I found, I used. It cost so mucl
trouble, and endangered so much "grumbling" t
introduce a new book into school, that I had no
the courage to attempt it.

In writing, we pursued the old mode, excep
that instead of writing the pupil's copy on his ow1
paper, I wrote, during leisure hours, a quantity o
copies on slips, and made use of them. I ough
before now to have mentioned, however, that
began, with every pupil, with the elements of let
ters, on the plan of Wrifford ; but as soon as m1
scholars had written a few pages of elements, i
was my custom, for want of time to do otherwise
to give them slips for copies, and leave them t
learn in their own manner. I did indeed pay then
some attention by going round and looking ove:
their shoulders ; but my superintendence was no
usually of much practical value.

Grammar and geography were pursued in 1
parrot-like manner. Nothing was done in then
to any purpose. Indeed the mere recitations whicl
I used to hear were not worth, even to the pupil
half the time which was consumed in hearin1
them. Arithmetic was taught as in my forme:
schools.

I had one or two young men in book-keeping

This was a branch of which I knew nothing myself. With the aid of a good treatise, however, and a little ingenuity, I succeeded in appearing to teach it.

My greatest success was in teaching my abecelarians. Excepting one,—a little girl under four years, whom I could not induce to speak aloud— they made very handsome progress. Sometimes I taught them separately, and sometimes in a class together. The latter method best pleased them, and was usually much the most successful.

In discipline, I met with a great deal of difficulty this year. I had several large boys—roguish by profession—whom I thought required occasional severity. On these, corporal punishment was sometimes inflicted. I do not say it did very much good ; but what else could I do ? They disregarded my rules, and set the school a bad example ; and I thought I had no time to take a longer and more rational method with them.

Once, I remember, I detained the son of a gentleman—whom I will here call deacon O.—after the close of school, at night, to punish him. He had never been accustomed to obey at home, and therefore knew not what obedience meant. The fault lay most with his father and mother, but as it would not so well answer the purpose for me to correct them, I corrected their son. This was quite as much as the deacon and his wife could endure; although they highly respected me. They thought, no doubt, I might have "sugared" over the matter, as they were accustomed to do, without resorting to the use of the rod.

On another occasion I punished, in nearly the same manner, a grand-daughter of the same family. She was a very bad girl, and I hoped the infliction of blows would save her and her companions from becoming still worse. I do not know that the punishment did her any good; but I believe it had a salutary tendency on the school. It arrayed the family against me, however; and though they outwardly approbated my conduct, it was easy to discover that their feelings were alienated.

The minister also had a boy who was full of little mischievous, though not malicious tricks. Him I punished, among the rest, though not very severely. I believe, however, that in doing it, I accomplished my object; and though it greatly wounded the feelings—perhaps the pride—of the parents, I do not know that they ever made any complaint.

The rod however was not often used; for I still retained, to some extent, the practice of boxing ears as a substitute. But I resorted sometimes to punishments, the very thought of which, even now, makes me shudder.

I had one little pupil—a lad—who, true to his own nature, and unwilling to sit so very still on the bench, was perpetually in motion, and some-times at play. There was no malice; but his de-sire for play was so strong that he found it diffi-cult to repress it. Poor fellow, how I pity him; and not him only but thousands in the same pre-dicament ! Compelled to " say A. B and sit on a bench " (as a certain writer has put into the mouth of a little boy who was asked what he did at school) for a whole hour at a time, it is no wonder they are restless. Their whole natures rebel. Adults would regard such treatment as downright tyranny were themselves subjected to it. As well, almost, might you confine the frolicksome lamb or kitten.

But this boy gradually became more than usual-ly restless, and troublesome. At last I threatened him with punishment. But no punishment came, though in forgetfulness the acts had been repeat-ed ; and the little fellow began to think nothing was coming. Alexander, said I, I will hang you up by your heels on that big nail at the end of the room, if you do not behave better.

The idea of being suspended by the heels was at first terrible ; and I thought I had now gained my point. But no ; even this threat was at last forgotten. He was at his old tricks again. Finally,

I began seriously to think of putting my threats in execution. So I tied my pocket handkerchief around his legs, at the ankle, and then fastened him by his heels to the large nail or spike as I had promised.*

I held him in that position a moment—for I did not dare to leave him thus suspended, or even to let go of him—and then took him down. The boy was not injured, that I know of; but he might have been. Such a punishment is altogether unjustifiable. Better, by far, as I have insisted elsewhere, to take a rod of proper size and chastise a child, than suspend him by his heels, even though it be but for a moment.

The punishment had its intended effect on the school, who were greatly frightened. As for the boy, he grew more cautious, though not less sly. I did not repeat the punishment, either on him or any one else; and I am glad of it.

No act of my life—so far as I know—ever ex-

---

* Many a reader will wonder why I do not suppress this fact. It is indeed terrible; but I did not, at the time, know anything of its danger. Having seen boys for sport stand on their heads, or descend a tree head downwards, it did not occur to me that holding him up so, a moment, was particularly dangerous. Of the fact that the boy's fright greatly increased the tendency of blood to the head, I was then totally ignorant. Let other ignorant teachers take warning.

14*

ited more of just and merited indignation against
ne than this.   It is true that report greatly mag-
ified the circumstances.   Still they were in them-
elves sufficiently shocking.   Yet the public in-
lignation was at length smothered, and, after
ome months, the act seemed to be forgotten.   It
annot be denied that my school, as a body, was
endered more passively submissive, by these acts
f violence ; but I think there was a loss of spirit,
nd of respect for me, and for themselves.   Their
ncreased silence and submission and passivity
vas obtained at too great a sacrifice.

SECTION V.

SCHOOLS NEGLECTED BY PARENTS.

One cause of the low state of schools.   Absorbing matters.   Love of money.   Love of distinction.   What
   in such circumstances is to be expected ?   My own
   expectations.   Disappointment.   What my wishes
   were.   The facts.   Parental visits, of little service.
   Reflections.

Experience had long before this time taught me,
hat one great cause of the low state of common
chools and common education was a want of inerest on the part of parents.   They had, indeed,

a confused sort of idea that they must have something in the shape of a school ; and that they must send their children to it, unless they had some apology for keeping them at home. They were indeed gratified—perhaps once a month—when a son came home with some badge of distinction for scholarship ; as well as sometimes dissatisfied, when their children—so excellently did they behave at home,—I mean in their own estimation—were censured or punished. But these were only *seasons* of interest. In general the current of their thoughts ran on something else, rather than the improvement of their children.

The more common and absorbing motive to action was the love of money. Respectability in society stood next. Distinction in civil office though open to all, in theory, was yet a practical life rather distant, except to a favored few. Attention to the fashions in regard to dress, house, furniture, equipage, as the means of respectability—and sometimes of wealth—occupied, next to money making, the most important place in the minds of many persons ; and in by far the majority engrossed nearly all their waking thoughts and conversation.

In a state of society like this, what can a teacher expect ? Could he—ought he—to hope for parental coöperation ? Ought he to expect the pa-

rent at home, even during the long winter eve
nings, to be helping his son forward over the diffi
culties of his lessons ?　And the mother aiding an
encouraging her daughters and sons both ?　Ough
he to expect them to inquire, with deep interest
after his health, and invite him in sincerity to com
and see them ?　Ought he to expect they wil
make the school room a place of frequent bu
pleasant resort ; and suggest to him, at a prope
time, the means of improving the condition of thi
or that class, or of moulding, in a better manner
the character and habits of this or that individual
Ought he, I say, under all circumstances, to expec
such treatment as this ?

And yet I did, at the time of which I am now
speaking, expect it.　I knew, full well, the importance of parental coöperation, and I though
that here I should obtain it.　I supposed that the
sacrifice I had made, in a pecuniary point of view
—the giving up of a year of my life to their service for a mere pittance, so far as the emolumen
alone was concerned—would arouse them ; and
that energy, and perservering and warm-hearted
efforts would continue it.　I thought they would
regard me as a doer of good to themselves and to
their children, and would take me by the hand
and help me onward.

But alas !　I had not yet read deeply our common nature. I did not know, as well as I now do, the power of habit. I did not know how paralyzing to every benevolent feeling, and to every virtuous or pious emotion, is the love of money!

Often did I invite the parents of children to visit us at our school room. Often did I beg them to come in at any time convenient, in their every-day dress. I pledged myself to show them our state and condition as a school, rather than to make a studied exhibition of the pupils, I abhorred the practice of " showing off" a school. Let that, as well as the visitors, I used 'to say, appear in its every-day costume.

I wanted the parents to visit us, and become interested in our proceedings, because I knew then, nearly as well as I now do, that until such is the case—until parents are awake to the importance of coöperating with the teacher—and to an extent, too, of which most of them have, as yet, never conceived—little can be done on their behalf. The world must continue to go on, much as it now is. The philanthropic teacher may sacrifice himself on the altar of the public good ; but it will be to little purpose.

A few parents—especially mothers—became slightly interested, at first, and I have already observed that it was through their interference, principally, that our benches were improved. But heir zeal did not hold out. It was zeal excited by sympathy ; not zeal " according to knowledge," as the Bible calls it.

They did indeed visit us ; but it was not heartily. They came in groups. One came, partly to accompany another. They came in an artificial manner, and gazed only at externals. I could not discover that one of them entered into the spirit of the thing. " It was very pretty machinery ;" they seemed to say, by their looks and by their words ; but this was nearly all.

When shall we learn, as parents and teachers, that these children, whom we deal with, are immortal ; that they have immortal souls ; that the great business of the parent is, to raise these deathless souls to excellence and happiness, here and hereafter ; and that the teacher is but a servant— a mere foreign assistant—called in to help them onward in their great work !

SECTION VI.

SCHOOL LIBRARIES.

Rewards. How conferred. Libraries substituted. Temporary usefulness. Remarks. Difficulties arise. Change of Plan. New Difficulties. Final disposal of the Books. General effects of mere knowledge.

In all my school keeping, up to the present time, I had been accustomed to reward meritorious pupils. This was usually done by giving those who were at the head of their respective classes, at the close of each week—sometimes at the close of each day—a small written or printed certificate. Sometimes this reward was bestowed on him who had been at the head of his class the greatest number of evenings in a given time or period—say two weeks.

The rewards as I have said, were conferred on the meritorious. By this I mean such as were considered at that time as meritorious. I had not then properly considered that this was altogether an unfair mode of proceeding. It rewarded him who possessed the best memory ; but not, of necessity, him who used his memory most during the time to which the certificate referred. It did not seem to regard good behavior at all. If the best speller were the worst boy in school, he must nevertheless, on this principle, bear away the palm.

This plan of bestowing rewards, now gradually yielded to another. I began, by degrees, to encourage reading among my pupils. And in order to this, I procured a library of small books, which I kept in my school room. Instead of giving certificates, I loaned books.

For a time, the plan seemed to work very well. It inspired me with new courage, at any rate ; and in this way one point was gained, if no more. It is very important for a teacher to feel as if all was going on well. So long as he feels *thus*, the very feeling insures, in a measure, his success.

Here is the secret of success, in regard to a great many new measures in school. It is our own confidence in them, that gives them their superiority. Let the best teacher in the world lose confidence in himself, or his own measures, and he is no longer the best teacher. On the contrary let a worse teacher *gain* confidence, and he has at the same time gained in skill. There may indeed be exceptions to this rule. There is such a thing as fool-hardiness in this matter, as in every thing else. But I have ever found, in my own experience, that when I enjoyed the best health, and felt the greatest degree of physical and moral courage, then — other things being equal — all things went on most happily ; that when I merely imagined things to be going worse, such would soon be their real tendency.

To return to the Library. All things, for some time, seemed to go on prosperously. At length it was found, however, that though a few were encouraged, many more were discouraged. I found that I was deemed partial in my favors, both by pupils and parents ; and, by some of the latter, unjust.

Another plan was accordingly resorted to. This was, to loan books to every pupil once a fortnight, or once a week. The only distinction to be made was, in letting those who had been at the head most—and for this purpose a record was kept—select their books first. This plan succeeded better than the former.

There was one great difficulty, which was to keep them from soiling, or otherwise injuring the volumes. Every district school contains some pupils who are wholly unfit to be trusted with books, unless parents will so far coöperate with the teacher as to watch over them. I had several of these pupils ; and as I had no parental coöperation, the books were soon dirtied, and defaced ; and of course, to the scholars, rendered uninteresting.

At the close of each winter school term, I was

15

accustomed to present these books to the pupils; and at the commencement of another term purchase a new set. It was an expensive business, but I thought it must be done; and for many years, I persevered in it. I am not however sure that, on the whole, it did much good.

I have elsewhere spoken of my great confidence in mere knowledge,—and especially reading—as a means of making both children and adults better. It was hard for me to get rid of this confidence. But I was at length compelled to abandon it. I found that neither children nor adults are necessarily improved,—or at least directly so—by all the mere knowledge in the universe. This did not lead me to neglect knowledge, but only to make more diligent effort to warm the heart as well as fill the head; and to elevate and direct the affections, as well as enlighten the understanding.

SECTION VII.

IMPROPER COMPANY. EXAMPLE.

An improper companion. Value of a friend. Relatives not always friends. Mingling in improper company. A set of semi-savages. The supper. An animal family. Evils of boarding round in families. Examinations of the school. Guessing. My real efforts. Getting sick. Recovery. Consequences.

During this year of my life, I committed several other errors: Some of them more, others less serious. I will relate them.

There was a young man in the neighborhood who came from my native town, and with whom I was already somewhat acquainted. His reputation was not very high; indeed there were evidently some sad defects in his character. Reluctant as I was to form new acquaintances, and yet extremely fond of society, I made frequent calls on this young man; and perhaps might justly have been regarded as intimate with him.

A kind female friend one day suggested the impropriety of my course; and advised me to withdraw from his society. I knew as well as she could tell me, that there was truth in the saying; "a man is known by his company." Still, for

reasons just given, I was unwilling to leave him.
I thought to do as I pleased.   I thought, moreover,
that my mountain of reputation stood strong, and
could not so easily be moved. I was not conscious
of any wrong intention in the association ; and
why, I said, should I trouble myself about what
others think ?

How much the young need wisdom, especially
at an age when they are so much exposed to danger! How valuable, at this period, are faithful
friends ! Would that I could have had but one !
Even one continued remonstrant would probably
have saved me from many errors and much
sorrow !

It is a lamentable fact that our best friends—I
mean our relatives, and more intimate acquaintances—are often of least service to us.   They flatter
us.   They are not faithful.   They do not persevere in their efforts to reclaim us.   They are too
much afraid of wounding our feelings.   This was
the case with the good lady whom I have just mentioned.   She gave me one hint, but finding I disregarded that, she gave up her purpose forever.

I do not dwell long on this point, because it is a
very painful one.   I do not know that I suffered
materially on account of this young man.   And
yet I might have done.   The risk I ran, was too
great.   I look back upon it with trembling.   It is

rue that a few families did lose a degree of their
onfidence in me, as I have since learned, but the
oss was not perceived at all at the time; nor
vere they families whose good opinion, in every
nstance, was of so much value as it might have
een.

Another error was the following. As I board-
d among the families of the district, there ap-
eared to be a necessity of my becoming, to a
ertain extent, all things to all. With this view,
sometimes mingled in society which was wholly
nfit for an instructor of children. I should have
aid, also, that it was a settled rule with me to
oard with every family who would receive me,
owever mean or worthless. Some teachers, by
eglecting to do this, had excited unpleasant feel-
ngs. This I was determined to avoid; and I kept
ny determination. No person could justly say of
ne, ironically; "He is too good to come and
oard with us."

In all this, I had regard chiefly to my reputa-
ion. I was determined to teach well, and to be
nown as a good teacher. I was determined to
e popular. And I succeeded in my object. But
t was a dear bought success; as we shall see in
he sequel.

I observed that I sometimes mingled with so-
iety unfit for me. There were several families

15*

whose sole happiness appeared to be in gratifying their animal propensities. They were laboring people, it is true, for they had no other way of procuring the gratification of which they were so fond, except by hard work. But whenever they received payment, they would, if possible, leave their work to have a frolic. Or if they could not be absent from the factory, would at least indulge largely in what they called good eating—oysters, lobsters, etc.

The men were passionately fond of hunting. There was indeed no game in that region worth pursuing; but no matter to them. If they could not find one species of animal to shoot, they could another. And what they killed, they always made it a point of honor to eat. Birds, squirrels, rabbits, mice, frogs, and even cats, if they found any abroad; in short, whatever they could catch, must be cooked—usually in the form of a soup—and wo betide him who would not partake of their good cheer, prefaced if not followed by alcoholic and fermented liquors!

It was my lot to be present at one of these—I was going to say *powows*, for it was more like a savage entertainment than a civilized one. I would have retreated, but it came upon me so suddenly that I had not time to muster a sufficient apology, for so doing; and I concluded to remain.

Their spirits and cider and other accompaniments I refused ; but I consented to take part in the supper. A screech owl was served out to me : which I found less difficulty in swallowing than I had supposed. It was indeed a slow process to masticate it ; but so much the better, as I was the longer well served ; and the less likely to be furnished with something still worse. I remembered the fable of the Fox and the Swallow. The noise and mirth and the general tone of conversation were not very edifying ; but the great evil of all was that here I found myself setting a most pitiful example to at least half a dozen of my pupils.

I also boarded at one place in the district where the moral character of the family was such as almost to ruin the reputation of a boarder, though was not fully acquainted with the fact, till I had spent a week in the family. The least inconvenience I suffered here, was that of living, during this whole period, chiefly on shell-fish.

This " boarding round," so common in New England, I now regard as rather objectionable because it subjects the teacher to all or nearly al the evils which I have named, and many more True it enables him to form a closer acquaintance with the parents of his pupils ; which is certainl an important point. But frequent visits to thei families would answer every purpose, equall well ; and would be, in many respects far preferable.

Our school was visited, this year, according to law ; and examined with a good degree of faithfulness. It was customary for the visitors to make reports on the state of the schools to the next subsequent meeting of their Board. I learned, with some satisfaction, that my own indefatigable labors were duly estimated. My school was represented as well disciplined, and instructed. I suppose the story of my *severity* did not reach their ears ; or if it did, it was doubtless believed to be exaggerated.

I recollect one anecdote which I heard from a source on which I could depend. The leading member of that portion of the Board who visited us, being asked how he liked our school, replied that it was excellent. " The master indeed," said he, " *guesses* a great deal ; but he usually guesses right." He alluded to the yankee habit I had acquired of saying at almost every breath ; I guess so or so. I was quite glad—ambitious as I was of distinction—that charges of no worse a kind were made, conscious as I was of sometimes meriting them.

Not that the minds of the pupils were not on the whole pretty well cultivated and expanded, for a term of one year. I do not think more had ever been done there in the same time—perhaps not as much. I had indeed gone, in some instances, quite beyond my strength. But then my miserable discipline—harsh, violent, and tyrannical—was more than the public sentiment ought to have endured. The sentiment of the district was rather old fashioned; and the excellence of discipline was, by the majority of the people, measured by its violence and severity—provided always that it did not affect them or their own children. Every one was very sure his neighbor's children needed whipping; but was more doubtful about the case of his own.

But the year passed away—its pleasures and its pains, its joys and its sorrows. Before the parting hour came, however, I was solicited to take charge of the school the following winter, to begin a month earlier than usual. I found they did not intend to continue my services through the summer; but the reason was, they thought they could not afford it. I did not learn that any individual objected to the continuance of the school through the summer months, except on account of the expense.

One circumstance in the history of this year at school, I have purposely thus far omitted, solely with a view to its relation in this place. The constant, unremitted efforts I had made, during the summer, to sustain the school, joined to other causes, brought upon me a fit of sickness in September, which came very near carrying me off. It was short, however, in its duration. I was restored to sound health in less than a fortnight, and returned to my school.

But though I recovered from this particular disease, I never recovered from the " wear and tear " of my constitution. However numerous my errors (and they were certainly neither few nor small) I doubt whether any person, with the same strength of body and mind—for I was not overstocked by nature with either of these sorts of vigor—ever made greater efforts than I did, in this district, and for the term of one whole year. No other five years of my life made such inroads upon my constitution. I was carried along, during this period, at least five years—perhaps ten—towards old age. Not for the sake of the trifling sum of $ 100 ; but to gain a reputation, and to do good. Reputation, however, was probably the main object.

CHAPTER VII.

MY SEVENTH YEAR.

SECT. I.

DIVIDED ATTENTION.

An anecdote. Change of purpose. Study of a new Profession. Its interference with my school. How it interfered.

The next October after I closed my session of a whole year, I was invited to take charge of the same school for the winter; or rather for six months. The price offered was eighty dollars, or nearly as much as I had received for the preceding whole year. This was quite an advance, both in regard to price and the duration of the term. It had not been common to extend the winter term beyond four or five months, or to pay a teacher more than twelve dollars a month for his services.

I was greatly encouraged, and accordingly made an engagement. Having gone through with another regular examination, I entered the school. Most of the pupils received me with open arms. There is something noble in the grateful attachment which children form for their instructors

ven when they are harsh and severe. It honors
uman nature. It is the more striking in the case
f district school teachers when we consider how
generally and entirely parents overlook and disregard them.

A circumstance took place at my examination,
which I am unwilling to omit both on account of
s general interest, and the bearing it has on the
articular subject of common school education.

At all or nearly all former examinations, we
ad met at a tavern, for this was the most conven-
ent place. When the examination was finished,
: had been customary to call on the landlord for
ome kind of spirituous liquor, as the fashionable
method of compensating him for the use of room,
ghts, and fuel. As the committee attended to
neir duties gratuitously, this little act of coutresy,
s it was called, was expected of the teachers.
These having procured the poisoned bowl, distribu-
ed it first among the committee, and then among
heir own number. What an example to set, by
company of teachers and a committee from a
Board of School Visitors, consisting of ministers,
physicians, justices of peace, and other distinguish-
d and influential citizens.

At the examination which I was now about to
ttend, in which I was joined by only one other
andidate, and he a strong temperance man, it

was resolved to make an inroad upon this long established but shameful practice. Accordingly when the examination was finished, instead of calling for spirits, we offered the landlord a reasonable compensation, and told the committee what we had done, and why we had done it. This committee of examination consisted of three persons; a minister, a physician, and a justice of the peace. They were surprised at the stand we took, and not a little chagrined, as it seemed like a reproach upon them. I was willing it should seem so; and hope it taught them a salutary lesson.

But to return to my story. The partial failure of my health, in consequence of severe efforts during the preceding year, had produced a partial change of purpose. I was still at heart, devoted to the cause of common education; but I was not without fears that I had not vigor of constitution enough to pursue it. It is a task which demands the mightiest energies of body and mind, notwithstanding the general opinion to the contrary; and even with these, few can endure it. Still I felt that the sacrifice ought to be made by somebody.

However, I resolved at length—though not without a great deal of reflection—to study another profession; in the hope that if I could not keep school, I could resort to that. It was a profession, by the way, whose study would, be a constant

16

reparation for the duties of a teacher ; both by the
eneral mental discipline it requires, and by the
articular knowledge it affords, in the manage-
1ent of minds and bodies of those committed to
ur charge.

I had always anxiously desired a liberal course
f education, but had been denied by poverty,
1e opportunity of procuring it. As I had now
ccumulated a few hundred dollars, and was as
et only twenty-five years of age, I availed myself
f the best substitute I could for a more liberal
ourse, and prepared to proceed with my studies.

It was, from the first, my settled determination
1ot to suffer my studies to interfere with the du-
ies I owed to the school. But they did actually
nterfere, in two ways. 1. They divided my at-
ention. He who has two paths to distinction be-
ore him, and intends to pursue either the one or
he other, according to circumstances, is not likely
o make as much progress in a given time, as he
vho not only has but one object in pursuit, but sees
1nly one path by which he hopes to reach it. 2. It
liminishes our energy. No man—I care not who
1e may be—can give his entire energy, especially
)f mind, to his daily employment, while he is study-
ng another profession.

It is true the school did not languish. I board-
1d from house to house, as before. I also swept

the house, and built the fires. I was there in the morning, and told the pupils stories. I was punctual, and the pupils were. We had even less corporal punishment in school than the year before. Still there was a want of energy. There was not that progress which after the efforts of the first year, ought to have been expected. There was " divided attention."

SECT. II.

TEACHING ON THE SABBATH.

I became a Sabbath School Teacher. This a wrong movement. Why. Three Reasons. Caution to teachers.

I attended a church on Sunday, where teachers were very much wanted in the Sabbath School. Although I felt very incompetent to the work of religious teaching, yet after repeated requests had been made, I consented to engage in the employment.

Whether my services were of any value to the minds or souls of those who came under my charge, I do not know. I only know that I was pleased with the employment. First, because in instruct-

ng others, I found myself instructed. Secondly,
because it satisfied in some measure the cravings
of an appetite which I had, not only to do good,
but to be *known* as a doer of good.——My pupils, I
had reason to believe, were also well pleased with
my instructions.

But I am now fully of opinion that the measure
was wrong. I wish to repeat and enforce the sentiment, that one thing—one important or responsible occupation—is enough for one time, at least
in any ordinary circumstances. It is—I repeat it
—my most deliberate conviction that we can never
have our district schools what they should be, until instructors are so employed and so paid that
they can sustain themselves and a rising family
solely by giving their undivided attention to this
one employment.

It is very natural, I know, as well as very common, to call upon the teachers of the schools to
assist in this benevolent work. First, because they
are supposed to have the art of teaching. Secondly,
because they have fewer engagements than other
people and less care, especially on Sunday; as
most of them are without families of their own.
Thirdly, because they are generally believed to
have a willing mind, and a benevolent heart.

I grant there is weight in all these considerations. Still I think that there are persons to be

found, not engaged in school ; either among parents or elder brothers and sisters—whose services would, on the whole, be nearly as valuable as those of the week day teacher.

But admitting it were not so, I should still insist that he ought to be excused. Nay, more ; I insist positively, that he ought not to engage, however strong may be his desires to do so. He cannot without injury to his body or his mind ; perhaps both. As this position may be doubted, I will give some of my reasons.

1. Because, I always found the " wear and tear" of my own constitution, in teaching, unaccountably great, whenever in addition to my own proper week day labors, I undertook to teach in the Sabbath School.

2. Because I have observed the same thing in others. There may be a few, so singularly favored in regard to vigor of constitution, that they can endure it ; but the number is very small. Where you find one of this sort, you will find fifty of the other.

3. Because God, in nature has not only ordained the Sabbath, but has so created us that we require that Sabbath as a day of rest. Not only is i necessary to man, but even to domestic animals But the teacher of a week day school, who goe into a Sabbath School, cuts himself off, in no smal

degree, from the enjoyment of that rest which God has not only prepared for him, but adapted to the wants of his whole nature.

These reasons, and many more, induce me to caution all teachers of week day schools—whether of a high or low grade—but especially the laborious teachers of infant and primary and common schools, to deny themselves any desires they perceive to be rising up in their hearts to engage in teaching on Sunday. Let them believe that God hath not only not required it at their hands, but in the arrangements of his Providence for our well being, has forbidden it.—Let them study to do nothing and to desire to do nothing which shall interfere with the main business before them. Let them attend to that whatever it may be ; and then do it heartily, as to the Lord, and not to man ; and then may they rest satisfied that they have done their duty.

I know not that anything further of particular interest occurred, connected with the well being of my school during this term. I heard no complaints this winter. But we separated, and as it proved in the result, to meet in the same interesting relation, no more.

CHAPTER VIII.

MY EIGHTH YEAR.

SECT. I.

GENERAL ACCOUNT OF MY SCHOOL.

A school offered me. Terms. Accepted. Character of my Charge. The colored boy. Resolution to preserve order. Punishment inflicted. Trouble with Pomp. Anecdote. Little accomplished this winter.

AFTER the close of my seventh winter in school, I gave myself up, almost without reserve, to the study of my new profession. The law required that it should be studied at least two years; and as I was now " the other side" of twenty-six, I thought it was necessary for me to go on with more rapidity than I had hitherto been able to do.

In the autumn, the gentleman with whom I studied became the district committee of the school district in which I boarded, and proposed that I should teach the school.

The compensation offered was about sixteen dollars a month; though I was to board myself. I accepted of the proposal; and, in due time, opened my school.

It was not large, but it was very unmanageable. It was the centre district; the pupils were rude ; usually ungoverned at home ; noisy, turbulent and vicious.   There were, indeed, a few noble exceptions; but they were few and far between.

Among the ungovernable class was a large colored boy.   He seemed to have little capacity for learning, though he was a boy by no means inactive.   He was extremely fond of fun and sport; and would, in his love for the latter, forget or seem to forget all of the rules of the school—no matter how good or how salutary.   So long as I could keep him employed in the school room, he did very well ; but the moment he was at liberty, his whole soul was so absorbed in play that he forgot everything else.   If he was told not to run across such or such a field, but to keep in the highway, he would, in the moment of temptation wholly forget it and venture beyond the limits assigned him.

I had several other ungovernable pupils, besides Pomp.   Some I punished ; others I kept in awe by the fear of punishment : and others there were whom I could scarcely manage in any way whatever.

In these circumstances, with a bad school on my hands, I thought I had but one course to pursue, which was to punish the leading offenders with great severity.   This I thought would awe the rest

into submission, and it probably might hav
done so, had I not carried the matter to an ex
treme that outraged the public opinion, and the
good sense of the community, in point of common
decency.

Several pupils were punished, corporally, and
with some severity ; and among the rest Pomp
But this made him the more violent. He was a
stout resolute fellow, and I was actually afraid o
him. Not that he was more than a match for me
if he had attacked me openly and directly. But
was absolutely afraid he would play the assassin

Still I was resolved to govern him, at some rate
and did so. It was, however, at great expens
—I mean of reputation. On his leaving the schoc
room one day I had told him not to do a certair
thing, in regard to which he had more than onc
disobeyed me ; but he had scarcely got beyon
the threshold, ere he was engaged in the very ac
which was prohibited. This was more than
could longer endure.

I cannot say that my anger was roused at al
but I felt a species of resolution take hold on me
and I was resolved to be master. I believed tha
the honor of the school law—and not so much th
pleasure of the master—demanded it. But I for
got that the honor of the school law and the digni
ty of the master, its executive officer, were a

closely connected in the minds of the pupils that
in lowering one, I must of necessity injure the other.   I forgot that, in sinking the character of the
master, I sunk the character of the school.

Near at hand lay a large—but not perhaps too
large—green rod ; and as soon as Pomp commenced his acts of disobedience, I sallied forth into the street, and pursued him.   Pomp could run
like a deer ; but I soon overtook him, and after
having inflicted several smart blows on his back,
without saying a word, I returned to my school-
room.

The affair was soon spread abroad in the neighborhood, and proved the occasion of many curious remarks ; but my character as a school teach-
was so well established and so favorably regarded
in a town where I had taught almost every winter
for six years, that the public were slow to believe I was as much in fault as I really was ; and
the matter at length died away.

Not a single improvement was made in methods
of instruction, or in discipline, during the whole
of this winter.   In fact the school was of comparatively little value to the parents or the pupils,
and may properly be regarded as a failure.
The circumstances which, added to my violence,
ended to this result, shall be developed in the next
section.

SECTION II.

CAUSES OF FAILURE.

The first cause. Neglect to secure parental coöperation. My purpose. My kind and affectionate treatment of small pupils. Second cause of failure. Too
many things at once. Third cause of failure. Too
little sleep. Its effects. A bad experiment. Remarks on sleep. Effects of too little sleep—on the
nervous system. Warning to teachers. Severe fit
of sickness. Causes.

The first cause of failure was a neglect to become acquainted with the parents of the pupils,
and seek and secure their coöperation. For the
fact that there is such an universal tendency in
people to overlook the district school, does not at
all lessen the teacher's obligation to awaken in
them such a degree of interest as will enable them
at least to understand what he proposes to accomplish ; and, in general, the kind and character of
the means by which he intends to operate. There
are, in fact, no circumstances, unless it were an
actual—" barring out " which justify a teacher in
remaining unacquainted with those whose children
are committed, for six hours, though for six hours
a day only, to his care.

All this, however, I had hitherto neglected. I

carcely knew half a dozen families, in the whole
listrict. More than this, I did not seek their ac-
uaintance. True, I invited them, through their
hildren, to call at the school room, but I did not
xpect them to come, nor were my expectations
ften disappointed.

My purpose was to go straight forward, and by
int of head-work—steady driving—make good
cholars, and good behaved boys and girls, whether
ie parents coöperated with me or not. All this
meant to do, peaceably if I could, but forcibly if
must.

It should have been mentioned, long before now,
iat in all my intercourse with my pupils, es-
ecially the younger ones, if they behaved well, I
vas deemed one of the kindest of teachers. They
ould not have expected more friendly treatment,
ven from a parent. I always wondered what
vas meant when I heard a teacher speak of diffi-
ulty in gaining the love of his pupils. It seem-
d to me one of the easiest things in the world;
nd to me it was so. The great trouble with me,
i this respect, was to retain, and preserve that
ive and confidence which, in my first intercourse
'ith my pupils, I found it so easy to acquire.

The second cause of failure was one to which I
ave already adverted as a former source of mis-
hief. It was the attempt to do other things. My

attention was divided, if not distracted.—I do not, I cannot—I am sure I never shall—approve of young men's attempting to teach, and at the same time pursuing the study of another profession. If a young man chooses to lay his studies wholly aside for the time—say during a college vacation— and teach a school, I have no objection. But let him, for the time, keep his books out of sight, entirely. Let him scarcely think of them.

Another, and a principal cause of failure was the following. Anxious to improve all my time, in the best possible manner, I had in company with a fellow student, resolved on sleeping no more than five hours in twenty-four. We retired at eleven and rose at four. This, I mean to say, was our rule. In my anxiety to rise at four, I often awoke and rose earlier; sometimes at half past three, and sometimes even by three. Sometimes too, though in bed by eleven, I did not get to sleep until ten minutes later. Under all these circumstances, I did not secure, upon the average, more than four hours of sound sleep in twenty-four. Nor am I sure that all this was *sound.* Anxious to awake at a certain hour, and fearful of oversleeping, I doubt whether our sleep is as sound and satisfying as when we yield ourselves up regardless of the future, and careless, or at least quiet, in regard to the past.

How much sleep is really needed, to sustain the
human constitution in its best condition, and to enable it to hold out in good condition, for the longest possible period, remains as yet, I believe, un-
determined.   There can be no doubt that we may
accustom ourselves, if in health, to almost any
amount not beyond twelve hours, provided we
manage in the appropriate manner.   The more
we sleep, and the less active our minds are while
awake, the more protracted does the season of repose gradually become, and the more sleep do we
seem actually to require.   On the contrary, the
more active the mind, during the day, and the less
our sleep, provided the amount is reduced very
gradually, the less do we appear to require.   I
have no doubt—nay I am certain—that I can bring
myself to find five and perhaps four hours amply
sufficient for the apparent restoration of enfeebled
nature.   I say *apparent ;* because a thing which
appears to be perfectly safe and harmless may be
laying the foundation of mischief twenty years
afterward.

I think that if the mind is sufficiently active—
if we obey, during our waking hours, all the organ-
ic laws, as Spurzheim call them—if we eat, drink,
exercise, etc., properly—if we retire by nine o'
clock, and rise as soon as the first nap is completed, we shall seldom, if ever, sleep too much.

This rule, however, will best apply to the healthy; for there are some invalids who are so much distorted, that they would not sleep enough at the first nap; while there are a few, who would, by the same rule, sleep too much.

In any event, myself and my companion erred in cutting short our sleep, to the extent of one or two hours, so suddenly. Indeed, I perceived the evil effects almost immediately. I used, even in school, to feel a drowsiness stealing over me. And when I was not drowsy, I was stupid or irritable. But I was too proud to give up the experiment. I thought to persevere in it as long as my companion. Besides, I expected, every day, to find nature yielding her unreasonable demands,— as I called them—and submitting to my new device for saving time. But nature knew her own business best, and was too strong for me.

I verily believe that the want of sleep affecting my nervous system, made me far more irritable in school than I should otherwise have been; and that I owed not a little of my trouble in regard to discipline to this very source.

Let this statement, and the facts which accompany it, operate as a warning to any young teacher who may chance to cast his eye across these pages. Next to attempting to perform too many things at once, let him beware of attempting to

urn night into day, with a view to save time. If
we succeed in cheating nature out of her just dues,
and all seems to go on well for a time, yet let us
remember that we must sooner or later return the
ll-gotten gain, it may be with usury. Man cannot become immortal at once. To reach the an-
gelic state—a state in which perhaps no sleep may
be needed—he must first submit to the laws im-
posed on flesh and blood. The road to immor-
ality, lies through the region of humanity.

But I have not yet done. While I was in the
full career of my experiments—at home and at
school—I was suddenly seized with an acute and
very violent disease. For a few days my life was
despaired of; but at length I slowly recovered.
My sickness, however, nearly broke up my school.
A vacation of six weeks had brought the time so
near the close of winter, that the remainder of the
season was of little value to my pupils.

How much my diminished sleep had to do in
the production of my disease, I do not know. It
might have aggravated it, and rendered it more
dangerous. The lady of the house, however, was
sick in the same way, and nearly at the same
time; and so were many other persons in the
neighborhood, and in an adjoining town. I doubt
whether my sleeping too little had much to do in
the production of the disease; though in this it is

quite possible I may be mistaken. However thi
may be, it was an experiment which I should no
dare to repeat.

17*

CHAPTER IX.

MY NINTH YEAR.

SECT. 1.

A NOVEL ENTERPRISE.

"Finishing" my Education. School keeping. Difficulties. Native Diffidence. Its causes. A favorite plan. Reforming my native town. Beginning with their schools. Want of a real friend. My efforts at improvement not a new thing. A fact in my history. Proposals. My proposals accepted. The school opened. Public surprise. Surprise of my relatives, and acquaintances.

WHEN I had completed the usual course of study and had obtained all those honors which were necessary to enable me to pursue reputably my new profession " in this or in any other country," I began again to think of school keeping. Indeed this was always nearest my heart. I had only resorted to another profession as a discipline to my mind, and that I might have, as the common saying is, " two strings to my bow,"—that is, that I might have, as a last resort, and in case of necessity, the benefits of a profession which though respectable I knew I could never love.

It was spring, and the summer was approaching. Few schools would employ male teachers at this season. But I was unwilling to be out of employment. I was indeed out of funds, and somewhat in debt ; but this was not a matter of great solicitude. I knew I did not owe so much but that I could, with economy, speedily pay it, in almost any occupation.

My health was not good, neither was it very bad. I was able to do something, and yet not strong enough—and consequently not morally courageous enough—to meet many difficulties, or encounter much opposition. How should I obtain a school, and where ?

I was particularly unwilling to go among strangers. You may wonder at this. A man with a college parchment in his pocket, you will say, so exceedingly diffident as that ! Strange, indeed —And so it was strange. But stranger things have happened. You have heard, no doubt, of the diffidence of the poet Cowper. He seems to have been a greater fool, in this respect, than I was.

Mine by the way, was something more than common diffidence ; although I was not then aware of the fact. It was a diseased state of feeling ; or rather it was that kind of timidity and irresolution which almost always accompany a person whose digestive powers and nervous system are in the state in which mine were at that time. In short I was consumptive and slightly dyspeptic—two states of the system, either of which is enough to bring down and make half idiots of strong and wise men.

At last I began to entertain hopes of hitting upon some plan for reforming my native town, not only in regard to its schools, but every thing else. It was a small, obscure place, but the people were negatively virtuous, and comparatively happy. They were a very simple people, and in this respect quite interesting. But they had little patriotism or public spirit, and still less benevolence. Every one lived almost independent of the rest; and it seemed to be an object with him to become quite so. Hence arose a degree of narrowness and selfishness which was rather unfavorable.

I thought if I could only elevate their schools to respectable standing, an important point would be gained. This I hoped I might do. My plan was to set an example of devotion to the employment of teaching a common school; to elevate the character of my own school, and then aid in improving the character of others. At the same time I hoped to encourage the circulation of books, magazines, papers etc., of which there was great need.

Had there been a real friend at hand, at this junction, who knew human nature better than myself; who could have taken me by the hand, and

pointed out, on the one side the probable assis
tance and coöperation I should be likely to receive
and on the other the difficulties which must inevit
ably be encountered, how invaluable would his ser
vices have been too me ! But no such friend was a
hand ; indeed I had none. At that period I ha
never had a true friend—a real one—although
had many relatives. They loved me *as* a relative
but could not sympathize with me, in any benevo
lent plans or projects ; because they were unac
customed to such enterprises. If any thing wa
proposed, they only discouraged me. They re
garded me as visionary.

My plans for the improvement of my fellov
townsmen were not a new thing. Nearly fiftee
years before this period, while quite a lad, I ha
made several unsuccessful attempts to start a l
brary for the young, in the same view which I nov
entertained, viz. the hope of slowly and silentl
promoting the public good. It is true I had mor
hopes of improving the condition of mankind b
mere *knowledge* than I new have ; still the thin
aimed at was neither more nor less than the ger
eral happiness.

I now thought seriously of commencing a schoo
somewhere in the town ; and, as if from a radiatin
point, to extend gradually my operations. I re
member telling one person to whom I had ventui

d to unbosom my feelings, that I hoped, one day, o see my native hills and dales vie with those of Switzerland.

The question came up, where should I begin, and how should I get a school? As I cared little or the pecuniary avails provided I received enough o support me, I offered my services to the central district of my native town; proposing to board in he families, and accept of six dollars a month, besides;—only a little more than they would be compelled to give a female.

The proposal excited some surprise; and why should it not? To see a man, after having taught school more or less ten years—received the highest, or nearly the highest wages—spent three years in professional studies—and received the honors of a distinguished professional institution; to see such a man come and beg the favor of teaching a district school at six dollars a month and his board, surprised them. They were unaccustomed to such things; and they could not understand what was meant.

They had little or no conception of the object I proposed to accomplish. Benevolence and philanthropy and even patriotism were names of which they hardly knew the meaning; and they were really as great strangers to the feelings which they imply, as to the names.

They held a meeting, however ; and it was not a little to my surprise, I confess, that they agreed to employ me. I was examined according to law, and received a license ; and I then prepared to commence my labors.

The school was opened in May. The appearance of a male teacher in a district school room, in summer, excited the attention, not only of my townsmen, but even of the passing stranger. Such a thing had been known occasionally, in some very large towns ; but never before in a small district, like this.

No persons were more surprised—and I may add mortified, than my relatives. They looked at me as a deranged person. Instead of taking my stand by the side of liberally educated men, and holding a station of command or influence, to go and place myself in a district school room at the head of twenty or twenty-five small pupils, and teach them the common, elementary branches of an English education—and all for the paltry price of six dollars a month—is it not inconceivable that they should have submitted to it ? Why did they not put me into a strait jacket, or carry me at once to a mad house ?

But the school went on ; and the earth continued to revolve, and the sun to shine as usual ; nor was there any thing in the physical condition of the universe, that indicated serious derangement, of any sort! People talked till they were tired of it, and there the matter rested.

SECTION II.

METHODS OF TEACHING. DISCIPLINE.

The first step at Innovation. Influence of the Journal of Education on my efforts. Ornamenting the school room. Teaching the Alphabet. Spelling. Defining. Want of proper School Books. Reading. Writing. Grammar and Geography. Arithmetic. Number of Exercises. An exercise in Thinking or Reflecting. Its uses. Discipline. Failure of my health. Breaking up of the school.

The first thing I'did that looked like innovation, was to get some paper curtains, for the windows. In this, I had two objects in view. One was to prevent the pupils from looking out, the other to ornament the room. I had already begun to think much of the importance of rendering a school room pleasant and agreeable ; and had been much aided in my speculations on the subject by the "Journal of Education," edited at that time by Mr. Wm. Russell. This work had been published about two years. I had also been greatly indebted to this work, not only for other views which I entertained, and which will be developed in the progress of this and subsequent chapters, but also, in no small degree, for what I possessed of the spirit of philanthropy.

Some little pains were also taken to ornament the walls of the school room. Maps were hung up, evergreens procured, and early flowers. Had I possessed the pecuniary means of doing it, I would have devised and executed plans for rendering the whole school house, both externally and internally, quite attractive.

In teaching the Alphabet to my pupils I do not remember that I devised or adopted any new plans. In fact I believe I had no abecedarians in my school. If I had, I feel confident I pursued the same humdrum method which had prevailed time out of mind, except that I probably taught them in a class, rather than separately ; in order to save time.—I had, it is true, many new notions on the subject ; but an imaginary want of time always seemed to compel me to resort to the old methods.

In regard to spelling, I was careful to assign my pupils short lessons, and see that they understood their meaning. This last was quite an innovation. Defining words as a school exercise, had then scarcely been heard of.

It is true we labored under great difficulties in

18

this matter of defining words, for want of suitable books. Here we came upon a department on which I had seldom, as yet, dared to place the " rude hand of reform." Our school books indeed, such as we had, I knew were sadly deficient; and in the department of defining we had none at all. A few of the older pupils had a very inferior sort of dictionary ; containing definitions which in themselves required defining ; but which were a little better for us than nothing at all; but the greater part of them were destitute even of this.

Had I possessed the means, I should have sent at once to a book store, and bought a set of some defining spelling book, and presented it to the school. But this I was unable to do ; and there is room for doubt whether such measures, however benevolent their intention, are, after all, judicious.

In reading, we pursued a course altogether new to the pupils. Instead of reading just so many chapters, or articles, or verses, each was required to read a small paragraph over and over, till he both understood it, and could read it with propriety. It was my usual practice however, to read it first myself, in every instance ; and sometimes, if the pupil was an unapt scholar, to read it over for him several times.

I did not find this method of reading so irksome to the pupils as I had expected. It is well known how fond children are of novelties; and so novel was our reading that for a few days it went off very well. But the pupils at length grew tired of it; and I found it necessary to resort, occasionally, to the old method. They probably found, in this, the appearance of progress. To stand still, as it were, at a single place in the book, for several minutes, seemed to them less like making improvement, than when they were reading off several pages at a single lesson.

But our lessons in reading were, in any event, short. I had got over, in some measure, the notion that the pupil's improvement was in proportion to the space run over. Sometimes, indeed, a large class read several pages at a time; but not usually. As a substitute for so much matter-of-course reading, I used to explain and illustrate things as we went on; and sometimes even to relate stories to the class.

Writing, instead of being pursued at all hours of the day, and under all circumstances, was confined entirely to the last half hour of the forenoon, and of the afternoon. This was allowing to each pupil an hour a day for the study of this art.

This plan, in regard to writing, is excellent. I know of one objection which can be brought against it. It is that many boys, in the winter, will, in this way, lose at least half their writing.

Their parents and masters are accustomed to permit, and even require them to leave the school at a certain time—frequently an hour before the school closes.

But to this it may be replied that in leaving school thus early, some lesson or other must be lost ; and most pupils can better lose the writing lesson than any other.

The suggestion, to teach writing at these hours and in this manner, I believe I first learned from Hall's Lectures on School Keeping ; an admirable work, which in my opinion no teacher ought to neglect.

In grammar and geography little was done ; but that little was performed in a rational and intelligible manner. It was not a mere recitation of words. The pupil was brought to feel that there was meaning in language ; and that there should be thoughts connected with it. In these branches, too, all our lessons were short.

Arithmetic was studied by a few, but not very thoroughly, on account of a seeming want of time. I had not yet come fully up to the belief —practically—that what is worth doing at all, in school, as well as elsewhere, is worth doing well ; and that it were far better that an exercise should be attended to but once a day or even once a week, than that it should not be understood. I still clung, at times and in certain things, to the old notion that there must be, every day, such a certain number of exercises; that the pupils must " read round," as it was called, twice in the forenoon, and twice in the afternoon of each day; and that there must be writing, and arithmetic, and grammar, and geography, and everything else going on, at least once in each half day.

Or rather, as perhaps I ought to say, I had not yet moral courage enough to innovate, in this respect, upon long established usages. Besides, I felt, as I ought to have felt, that all improvement must, from the nature of the case, be gradual.

There can be but two advantages in " going round twice," in each half day with the reading and spelling exercises of our district schools. The first is, that it prevents ignorant teachers from imposing as long lessons upon pupils, as otherwise they would; the second, that it breaks in upon the disagreeable monotony which might otherwise prevail, and which commonly does prevail in the best common schools.

But were every child furnished with pleasant employment, and with suitable seasons for exercise in the open air, the second class exercise might far better be spared. Let there be but one exercise in each class in half a day; and let that be thoroughly attended to. I am here speaking

18*

of spelling, reading, and writing.   As to arithmetic, grammar and geography, it is quite enough that they come once in a day.

Our religious instruction consisted merely in repeating portions of the " shorter catechism," at the close of the week.   An example of daily prayer was indeed set, and the older classes read in the New Testament as a regular exercise ; and I was accustomed to moralize on daily occurrences. This last is probably the most effectual way of religious teaching in our district schools ; as it is in the first place, the most agreeable to the pupils ; in the second place, least likely to awaken, any where, sectarian jealousy ; and in the third place, most effectual in reaching the heart ;—and lastly, the impressions are the most permanent.

One exercise was introduced into this school, which, for anything I can now recollect, was altogether of my own invention.   It was a sort of silent, or thinking exercise.   After the school had been opened a short time in the morning, and my oldest or first class had read a Testament lesson, they were required to devote a certain number of minutes, usually from five to ten, to reflection. No scholar might attend to business of any kind whatever, during the time ; but all were required to observe the most perfect silence.

When I announced that the time was expired,

they were required to be able to tell me what had been done by their own class the preceding day. In some instances, I found them able to give a pretty faithful narration of all the exercises, and of many observations and illustrations of my own at the time. With a little aid, by way of questions and suggestions, I could usually draw out a pretty full history of their progress. They were also desired to state any errors they might have made, or defects they had observed ; not only in themselves, but in me, as their teacher. They were thus led to profit, on every successive day, by the errors of the past.

Had the school been continued long enough, I believe this exercise would have been of great value. As it was, it was worth something. It would have been worth more had I succeeded in convincing my pupils—which I had not time to do fully—of its vast importance in leading them to the daily habit of reflection, out of school as well as within.

In the discipline of the school, nothing occurred which is worth relating. I did not succeed entirely in dispensing with corporal punishment ; though I believe nothing was done which could have been construed, by any one, into severity or tyranny.

In short, we had made, on the whole, a prosperous beginning. The scholars and parents were, I believe, in general satisfied, and some were highly pleased ; and I was greatly encouraged. But nothing in this world, it seems, is stable and certain. My health failed after the school had been continued about six weeks, and I was forced to abandon the experiment, and, as it eventuated, resort to another profession.

CHAPTER X.

MY EXPERIENCE AS A SCHOOL VISITOR.

SECT. I.

EXAMINATION OF TEACHERS.

Change of Employment. Engaged in a new profession. Am appointed a school visitor. First attempt at Improvement. Second point to gain. Low standard of qualifications for teachers. Causes of this state of things. Attempts to raise the standard. Only partial success. Reasons. Some peculiarities in our examinations. Effects. Little, on the whole, gained. Results to ourselves. Men do not alter much after forty years of age.

IT will be seen by the closing remarks of the last chapter, that I had been forced to abandon school keeping on account of my health, and in order to regain it, resort to another profession. It was a most painful event to me, but it was one to which I was forced to submit. From the knowledge I had of my disease, and from the advice of the most judicious physicians, I was fully convinced that no other course would restore me.

Accordingly I set up in the early part of the following autumn, in the business of my new profession. I was soon appointed one of the Board of school visitors, whose office, in that State, was not only to *visit* schools, but to examine candidates, and grant licenses.

My first attempt at change, in the mode of examining candidates for teaching, was to induce the Board to hold stated meetings for examination, and give notice of the same. The object was, first, to accommodate the candidate, who often found it difficult as well as painful to his feelings, to go about town and collect persons to examine him; and secondly, to save ourselves time and trouble. I did, however, but partially succeed.

The next effort was to raise the standard of qualifications in the candidate. Hitherto, although it was no longer ago than the year 1828, it had only been required of teachers to understand spelling and reading, and a little arithmetic; and to be able to write a good hand. As to grammar and geography, they had seldom, if at all, been mentioned in the examinations of teachers. The reasons for this were as follows.

1. Grammar and Geography were very little taught in the town; although there were at least seven districts; embracing, one would think, some hundreds who ought to understand those branches. When either of them was taught, it was taught in a very superficial and slovenly manner; and it

was never made a subject of examination by th
Board of visitors at their official visits.

. 2. The candidates who presented themselve
for examination did not understand those branches
and therefore had they been made an indispensa
ble requirement, no teachers could have been ob
tained. How could they be expected to under
stand these branches ? They were labbring youn
men. They had •been brought up on the farm
and'as there was no regularly kept school in tow
of a higher grade than the district sohool, and a
their parents had been unable, in a pecuniar
point of view, to send them abroad, they had gen
erally enjoyed no opportunity of studying anythin
but the common and narrow routine of their na
tive district school.——I say *generally*, because th
minister of the parish sometimes taught a fev
scholars during a' part of the winter ; but even thi
school was deemed by the greater part of the in
habitants as too expensive.

And yet it was a well known fact, that asid
from their inability to instruct in branches whicl
they did not understand, the teachers of this town
taken from the plough, as they were, made th
best teachers in all that part of the country, and
were much sought for in all the adjoining towns
where the advantages of high schools were mor
common. This is only to be accounted for by

supposing that their industrious and enterprizing habits—for they were truly industrious and energetic—gave them a force of character which was not common among their less industrious neighbors. What they undertook they usually persevered in ; and what they did, in general and to a certain extent, they did well.

3. The Visitors themselves, generally, unless perhaps the minister of the parish, did not understand either grammar or geography. This was of course, a very obvious reason why they should avoid an examination in those branches. They would not like—of course—to expose their own ignorance.

4. There was a general belief abroad, as I have mentioned elsewhere, that it was useless for a teacher to understand a branch which he did not teach. That there was no necessity, for example, of understanding grammar or geography, in order to teach reading. I have heard this opinion, in substance, gravely stated and maintained in that same region, by intelligent men, as lately as the year 1829 or 1830. Strange error !—one which it seems no thinking person could ever make !

Every day's observation shows us that reading may be taught—and with much success too—by those who are ignorant of the grammatical construction of the language. I have just mentioned stri king cases in support of this position. And yet nothing is more certain than that however skilful and successful a teacher is without this knowledge, the same teacher would be far more successful and skilful with it. This remark is *especially* applicable to the study of grammar as a preparation for the business of teaching to read; but it is an undoubted fact that there is no knowledge which can be acquired in the whole circle of human science, which is not in a greater or less degree useful in qualifying a person to discharge the humblest duties of the most obscure country school master.

Fully convinced of this, I sought to make it a point to require our teachers to understand grammar and geography, whether they were expected to teach them or not. The point, however, was only partly gained. It was indeed acceded to by the Board; but when we came to the application of the principle; we shrunk back; which soon rendered it a dead letter in our record book.

The truth is, as we have already seen, the several districts were accustomed to employ teachers from our own town; and had we rejected their favorite candidates because they fell short of a new standard we had raised, they would have been compelled, in most cases, to go abroad for their teachers, to other towns. And where was the necessity, they would have said, for the change

19

Our schools have gone on very well these many years, on the old plan; why not continue it?

To have shown them that though their schools had gone on very well, they had not been at all improved; that while every thing else had been advancing, district schools had remained stationary, if they had not actually retrograded; and that there was an absolute necessity of going forward —making some advances—in this matter; why what good would it have done? Just none at all. To refuse to license their candidates, though we could show them that they fell short of our standard, did not succeed either. It only raised a tumult. What was to be done?

I can tell you what *was done*. For the sake of peace, we yielded our principles. True, I was the last to give up; but after holding out a good while against the public sentiment, I at length consented to yield and license such men as were brought us, provided they came up anywhere near our former standard.*

---

* I remember one very curious instance of examination. The district, fearing their candidate would not be licensed, had deferred an examination till the close of the school. Then as they were not entitled to a share of the public fund, until she had been licensed, they presented her for a license; and she was examined by being asked how to spell a single common word, and duly licensed! So little was the spirit of the statute

There were, however, certain other points o
which I still insisted, in our examinations. Or
was to see that the candidate had a thoroug
knowledge of the branches in which he was exan
ined. In orthography, for example, it was n
sufficient that a teacher could tell what sound
had in the second syllable of the word *acquai*
tance, but also what sounds it had in the other sy
lables, together with the sounds, both of the vowe
and consonants, throughout the word.

We also inquired in what way—if he had neve
taught school—he intended to secure good orde
and proper discipline ; in what way he proposed t
teach manners and morals ; whether he woul
consider it a part of his duty, to consult the healt
and happiness of his pupils out of school as we
as in it ; whether he thought it important to kee
young pupils employed ; and many other poin
of equal importance and prominence.

These inquiries however—novel and unprece
dented as our course of proceeding was—did no
very well go down. Some thought they wer
wholly irrelevant ; others that they were very wis
and learned ; others still that they were too rigid
The great difficulty, however, was, that they wer
matters on which new candidates had seldom ex

adhered to, and so barefaced were our evasions of it
for the sake of peace, and our purses.

pended a thought; and about which they had no particular care or anxiety.

The final result was, that, after all our efforts, the schools were fitted out for the winter with nearly just such teachers as those to which they had formerly been accustomed. Indeed, I do not know that we ever made the least degree of progress, except among ourselves. Some members of the Board were, I believe, often instructed by the course which was pursued; or at least they were convinced of our former, as well as present errors. This indeed was a point gained, had it been maintained.

But most of us were arrived at a period of life, at which opinion, and especially practice, seldom undergoes much change. School Visitors at forty years of age, if ignorant and shortsighted, will generally remain ignorant and shortsighted still. Put them in possession of a new or important principle to day, and they seem to lose it again to-morrow. The old associations of ideas resume their sway again; and every favorable impression or hope of progress is swept away like the traces of the traveller in the sands of Sahara.

No; the world has little to hope, in the way of improvement, from men forty years of age, unless they have already commenced a wise course of improvement. In that case, everything is to be

expected from them. They have lost little o
their capacity for action, while their gain, in wis
dom to direct that action, has been immense.

SECTION II.

SPECIAL VISITS TO SCHOOLS.

Requisition of the Statute. Neglect. Hurried visit
Superficial visits. How usually conducted. My ow
efforts. Visiting alone. My case not singular. Thi
duty often thrown on Ministers. My attempts to b
thorough. Results. My course unpopular. Excej
tions. Tribute to female worth. One female teacl
er desirous of Improvement. Her health injured i
a bad school house.

We were required by the laws of the State, t
visit each school at least twice ; one of which visil
was to be near its commencement, and the othe
near its close. This requirement of the statul
had, in general, been but partially complied witl
The winter school had indeed, for the most par
been formally attended to ; but the summer scho
had been frequently neglected.

But in all cases the visits had been hurrie
They had degenerated to a mere ceremony. The
consisted chiefly in hearing each class " rea
and spell" a little—occupying in the whole from

three quarters of an hour to an hour of time. No questions were asked in arithmetic—none in grammar—and geography. If the time admitted—which seldom, however, happened—they were expected to repeat the Introduction to the Spelling Book, the abbreviations, the pauses, and a few other matter of course things.

Even these examinations were often made under unfavorable circumstances. Instead of making the first visit during the first or second week of school, and the other near the close, as was the intention of the law, and as was indispensable in order to be able to judge of the progress which had been made, it was not unusual to defer it to the end of the first month; and sometimes even to the second.

The lessons, too, especially in reading, were very unfair specimens of progress. They were usually selections which had been read ten or a dozen—perhaps twenty—times over, and which each pupil knew, or almost knew, by heart. It is true the Visitors were empowered by law to require them to proceed in such a manner as they pleased; but this right had seldom been exercised. Even if the teacher invited them to select the pupil's lessons, they generally refused. In short, the visits were a mere formality; and were felt to be such by all parties concerned.

Such was the state of things when I became member of the Board. In some respects, indeed it was still worse than I have represented. When we came to divide into classes our four visits, was difficult to find any who would pledge themselves to a prompt and faithful performance of duty—a point which I considered indispensable The result was that I visited all the schools mysel and very frequently alone.

My lot was not wholly singular. It was no uncommon for some minister of a parish—fo ministers, though not always the best judges o common schools, were usually appointed to the office of Visitor—to be driven to the same neces sity. Either the visits must be omitted, or he must have philanthropy enough to make them alone. True, this was an evasion of the letter o the law, which required at least two members o the board to be present on such occasions; bu then it was a kind of evasion which was tolerated

For my own part, I not only visited the school myself, but I endeavored, at first, to examine them in a proper manner. At the first visit, I did no indeed attempt to accomplish much. It was my object to be a mere passive spectator. At the second visit, however, I endeavored to pursue a course which would determine the degree of im provement actually made.

But I found such a course of proceeding very unpopular. The teacher was not pleased with it ; the pupils were not pleased with it ; the parents were not pleased with it. They deemed me too authoritative. Even my companion in office—when I was so fortunate as to get one—had doubts *whether the public sentiment would bear us out in attempting anything like thorough improvement.*

.The point was at last partly yielded ; and the teachers were suffered to pursue their own course. I will not say that no good was done ; for it is impossible to say how far it is useful to stir up the public mind to this subject, even though we encounter opposition by it.

One important point had however been gained, especially with some of the female teachers ; and I mention this to the honor of the female character. They had become convinced, by my general conduct, as well as by my questions and remarks, that they were not doing, in their schools, all which might be done. Several of them were led to inquiry. And had suitable means been afforded them at the time, I have no doubt they might have been led on to a high degree of improvement. But I was unable to furnish them with the Journal of Education—the best work of which I then knew, to open their eyes—nor even with Hall's excellent Lectures on School Keeping. To

one or two of them I loaned Miss Edgworth
Practical Education ; but their minds were as y(
too immature—I mean in this department (
study—to derive much benefit from it.

I remember one young lady, in particular, wh
begged hard for information. She said that on tl
whole subject of conducting a school she felt tl
most profound ignorance, and that she had ever
thing to learn. She was indeed, sometimes temp
ed to leave her profession ; and she only remai
ed in it, as a choice of evils.

Such a spirit is the true preparation for progres
It is a sign of improvement, says Dr. Watts, wh
we begin to perceive how weak and unwise v
are. This young lady, notwithstanding her sen
of her own deficiency, kept a comparatively e
cellent school ; and often taught both winter ai
summer. I do not know that she would have r
linquished the business to this day, had she not
shattered her physical constitution, by her effor
that she was compelled to do it. She had be
teaching a winter school in a cold, bleak plac
and in a very bad school house ; one in which tl
floor was so much neglected that considerah
currents of air came up through the crevices, ai
produced disease. A severe cold terminated in
fever ; and this, with doubtful, or wrong medic
treatment, put an end to her school keeping

that season, and destroyed much of her vigor for life.

SECTION III.

MEETINGS FOR IMPROVEMENT.

Efforts to improve teachers. Meetings once a fortnight. Not successful. Inquiry into the causes of failure. Probably my own mismanagement.

During the first winter after I became a member of the Board of School Visitors, I made a strong effort to do something to promote the improvement of the teachers. They were mostly young men of my acquaintance, and seemed willing to unite in any plan which promised to add to their usefulness.

The plan I hit upon was to invite both the teachers and the Board of Visitors to meet, once a fortnight, for conversation and consultation in regard to the best methods of teaching and managing a school. With a view to afford every facility in my power, I furnished a room for the purpose.

We had one or two meetings at first, which were not without interest. But either my own mismanagement or some other cause was in the

way of their persevering. ˙ The number of botl
Visitors and teachers gradually diminished, so tha
it was not thought advisable to continue the meet
ings.

I spoke of my own mismanagement; for
strongly suspect that my zeal—untempered as i
was with that knowledge of human characte
which is so necessary to success in an undertakin;
of the kind—defeated my own plans and purposes
I am now quite of opinion that my associates con
sidered me as officious and rather overbearing
if not quite too much given to innovation. The;
considered me a *bookish* man ; one who mean
very well indeed ; but one who knew nothing o
men and things.

Now it requires a great deal of wisdom to man
age these things, in the world, and not defeat ou:
own best and dearest purposes and intentions
" Be ye wise as serpents and harmless as doves,'
said He who knew what was in the human heart
to a number of his disciples one day, in sendin;
them out on an important mission. And oh, how
necessary is the same wisdom and inoffensiveness
in all the departments of human effort ; especiall;
wherever and whenever anything is done whicl
savors of innovation upon established customs
habits and manners !

SECTION IV.

INTRODUCTION OF A NEW READING BOOK.

Reading Books in the Town.   Their general character.
Why new books were needed.   My own views of reading books for schools.   A new book at length introduced.   Its effects.   Objections to it.   Their frivo-
lous character.

An attempt was also made to introduce better
school books, especially as reading books.   Most
of the schools had been confined to the New Testament, the American Preceptor, the English Reader, the Columbian Orator, or Webster's Elements
of useful knowledge, for a long series of years.
Indeed there was scarcely a pupil then in the
schools who had ever known, in his own day, any
change.   Some of these books are respectable
books for higher classes; but others are hardly
suitable for any.   But good, bad, or indifferent,
they were read with no sort of interest; and I was
extremely anxious to introduce some new book,
which, while its tendency and style were excellent,
should at the same time please the pupil.

Long experience in teaching had shown me,
what the experience of every teacher and parent
must inevitably confirm, that children will make

twice the progress in learning to read from a boo
which is in some measure intelligible to them, tha
from one whose style and sentiments are beyon
their capacity or their years.

I am far from being friendly to that affectatio
of childish simplicity in the style of some of ou
children's books which has become of late so com
mon.   A real child-like style is like any othe
style, except that a choice of words is made whos
meaning is a little more obvious.   There is a
adaptation of idea rather than of language to th
child's apprehension.   A boy who will not unde
stand a very eloquent speech, which he reads in
school book, will understand nearly the sam
words of the language arranged in the form of
simple story, or an account of some person, place
or animal.   The reason is plain.   In the forme
case, the subject is one on which he has no
thought.   He has not yet entered upon politic
In the other—the latter—instance, he is more o
less familiar with the subject ; and hence the sam
words, in their appropriate combination, are quit
intelligible to him.

After much conversation with teachers and oth
ers, an effort was made to introduce into all th
schools in town a new reading book.   It was prin
cipally designed for the middle classes ; bu

neither the older nor the younger were to be prohibited its use.

The children were pleased with the book, and it answered, in many instances, a valuable purpose. I believe more real progress was made in reading, through its instrumentality, in one year, than had been made in two years before.

Still it did not give entire satisfaction to the parents. It was a story book.* And although they were no less deeply interested in its perusal at home, than their children were at school ; though they loved its simplicity, and wept at the moral lessons it conveyed, yet—what? Oh, it did not seem to them like a very good school book. They could give no reason for the feeling ; they could only say it *seemed* to them so. And such was the opposition to it, that it finally went into disuse, in most of the schools. Not, in most instances, sooner than it ought to have done, it is true ; provided its place had been supplied, as it should have been, with another. The practice of reading the same book in a school, year after year—I had almost said century after century—is very bad policy, and no better economy.

There was one man—a political opponent of my own—who, by his sneers, did more to destroy

* Story of Jack Halyard, the Sailor Boy, by Mr. CARDELL, a distinguished teacher.

the influence of the book, and to discourage the practice of often changing our class books for reading than any other person. He thought the child ought to read a certain sort of books—the very books which had been so long in vogue—whether they understood them or not. A strange mistake! And yet it is a very general one.

CHAPTER XI.

MY TENTH YEAR IN SCHOOL.

SECTION I.

COMMENCEMENT OF SCHOOL.

Left my profession for School keeping. Reasons. My Situation. School Funds—Their tendency. School house. Arrangements. Number of Pupils. My prospects. Expectations concerning me. One source of apprehension. Apology.

AFTER spending three years in my new profession, and recovering my health, I began to think of abandoning it, and returning, once more, to school keeping. Not from any want of success in the station I then occupied, for perhaps few have been more fortunate, but I had the following reasons.

1. My mind was prone to dwell, with great pleasure, on the idea that I was born for the purpose of improving the condition of my fellow men. But there were difficulties where I now was which seemed at present, insurmountable. There were deep founded prejudices, which I could not hope to remove, or live to see removed by others.

2. My health was fully restored; and I believe I had now learned the art of preserving it.

3. The professional studies in which I had en gaged were of such a nature as had led me to thinl more and more, of the importance of commo schools, and the indispensable necessity of impro ving to the highest possible pitch, every form c elementary education and instruction.

Having therefore made the necessary arrange ments, I quitted my station, and in ten days, foun myself once more in a district school. I need no tell you, perhaps, that I felt more real joy in th exchange than most seniors in college would fee on being appointed to the presidency.

I had placed myself—tho' only a few mile from home—among strangers. Yet it was a pleas ant neighborhood; and had some advantages ove many others. The schools in that region, as wel as elsewhere in the State had been much injured by an unconditional school fund; which, in dis pensing its favors pretty liberally, had graduall} led people to rely almost solely upon it, so far a there was actual need of applying money; and tc put forth no exertions of their own. And he who knows anything of human nature, knows full well that no people, in such circumstances, will long re tain much interest in the school which is thus, as it were, supported by a foreign power. However,

20*

I have spoken of the evils of funds in the first chapter.

But in the district in which I had now engaged, it was otherwise. They had been in the habit, from year to year, of taxing themselves to a considerable extent, especially for the support of their winter schools. The result was, that they had not only retained a stronger feeling of interest in the school than many other districts were accustomed to, but they actually had better schools. They not only paid a price somewhat larger, but they continued the school longer. And while it lasted, they visited it more.

The district was very compact, and very pleasantly located. The house, though not large, was on the whole good. It consisted principally of the school room and an entrance. It was well warmed and lighted. It was indeed, on a public road, and very near several mechanics' shops, besides a number of dwelling houses. Still it was rather a pleasant location for the winter, though not so pleasant for summer.

The number of pupils was about forty; and they were of all ages, from three to twenty. I engaged for four and a half months, at fifteen dollars and my board a month. Of course I was required to walk around the district, and board in the families. I opened my school early in November.

Here I had resolved on a grand experiment, in school keeping; although I meant to begin cau tiously. It was not my intention to attack or eve seem to slight old usages. My object was t change the spirit of the school, rather than to in novate largely upon its forms.

No stranger ever begun a district school wit better advantages—everything considered—tha I did, on this occasion. I had the prepossession of the people in my favor, with one exception; t which I shall refer presently. They had nearl all heard of my former reputation, as a teache as a citizen, and as a professional man; and wer therefore prepared to hope much—perhaps to much—from my exertions. I was prepared, to from what I had heard of them, to expect a goo degree of coöperation and support.

The exception which had some weight with portion of the people—to which I have just referre —arose from the consideration of my sudde leave of the profession in which I had for thre years been engaged. There I was, and, as it wi generally supposed, doing well, and "makin money"—the latter, you know, answers all thing in a world like this—when of a sudden, I was he soliciting a school. What could it mean?

Although I told them, in simplicity, how th matter was; yet they did not all seem to unde stand me. Nor was it to be wondered at. My best friends and nearest relatives did not understand why I should take such a course, although a few of them had long known I contemplated it. The idea of *descending*—for so it seemed to them —to take charge of a district school, at fifteen dollars a month, they thought very strange indeed ; and not only strange, but unjustifiable. I had scarcely a friend in the world who did not both wonder and disapprove. What else could have been expected then, of strangers ?

I have entered into these particulars because they have some bearing on the history of my progress during the winter. It is obvious to every reader that I was likely to be closely watched ; that while the majority were prepossessed in my favor, there were some who might strongly suspect me of a slight degree of mental aberration. Indeed a charge of this kind, in one or two instances, had been already cautiously preferred.

However, as I have already observed, I was now in my school, and my scholars around me. Everything seemed to go on pleasantly, and to promise us a season of much happiness and mutual improvement.

SECT. II.

SPELLING, READING, WRITING, ETC.

How the spelling was conducted. Writing. Arithme
tic. Evening Schools. Assistance given morning
and evenings. School Libraries.

All my pupils, as is usual in district schools
attended to spelling and reading ; and nearly al
of them to writing. I had also a very consider
able number in arithmetic, grammar and geogra
phy. Defining and Composition, moreover, re
ceived a degree of attention, especially the former
But of this last and grammar, I shall speak a
length in other places.

The spelling and reading were conducted in an
appropriate and rational manner, except. that, a
first the lessons were rather too long. But I soon
made them shorter, and paid more attention t
the manner of their recitation or performance.

In spelling, I took great pains to pronounce
each word as it should be pronounced, in good
speaking or reading. It was quite customar
with young teachers—and it must be confessed
with some old ones—in that region, to pronounce
the word, if possible, in such a manner that the
pupil could not fail to perceive nearly every letter

even though it were at the sacrifice of the true sounds of those letters. Thus instead of pronouncing the word *regency*, as we pronounce it in correct conversation, with the second and third vowels short, it was customary to say regen'cȳ ; making the *e* in the second syllable so plain that the child need not be in danger of substituting *i* or *u* or *io* for it; and the *y* so plain that it was impossible to mistake that for anything, unless it were for *i*. This wretched practice I had always avoided; but especially did I avoid it this winter.

Nor did I confine the pupils to columns of words, as arranged in the tables. Sometimes I gave them a reading lesson to spell, requiring them to study thoroughly all the hard words they could find in it. A thousand little devices were used to interest them in the exercise, which it would take up too much time now to name. In short the grand point was to make it a rational, rather than a purely mechanical exercise.

Writing was attended to, as in a former school, at the close of each half day; and half an hour was the usual length of each exercise. This plan for teaching writing, in a common district school, is the best I have ever tried; and I can cheerfully commend it to those who have never departed from the old plan of having it going on at all hours, and in almost all ways and circumstances.

Arithmetic was pursued, this winter, in the old fashioned manner ; except that I saw more and more the importance of encouraging each pupil to study everything out himself, instead of going to his fellow pupils, or to the teacher, for aid. I urged it on them all to be thorough, as far as they went ; and I sometimes put forth questions to them, to test their profoundness.

We had a few evening schools for arithmetic, by particular request of the pupils ; but I always avoided them when I could. Not that I was unwilling to devote myself entirely to their service ; but because I had reason to doubt both the motives of those of the pupils who were the loudest petitioners on the subject, and their practical utility whenever they were permitted.

I did not hesitate, however, to devote a reasonable measure of attention to any pupil in arithmetic, who wished to study at the school room at any other hours besides the six devoted to school ; and as I was usually there, a long time, both before and after school, a few availed themselves of the opportunities thus afforded them.

I had this winter, a very small collection of books which I was accustomed, occasionally, to lend to my pupils ; but it did not constitute anything like a regular library. I had grown a little tired of libraries, in the school room ; but it was chiefly, I confess, on account of the expense. I still believe that, with judicious management, they might be made to have a good tendency.

SECTION III.

TEACHING GEOGRAPHY.

An improvement. Description. Progress. Effects of this kind of Instruction. A caution to parents and Teachers. Spirit of this method infused into the School.

In the study of Geography I flatter myself that I made quite an important change this winter. True, the recitations went on, in school, much in the old manner, except that the lessons were rather short, and I endeavored more than formerly, to make them thoroughly understood. But I had formed and adopted, for myself, a method of teaching the elements of this branch—sometimes at home, sometimes at school, which was certainly an improvement, because it was something which was highly indispensable to the right preparation of every young mind for the study of this important science.

I usually commenced by showing my pupil or pu-

pin, some very small object which I had about me
or which they had about them—one at any rate
with which they were perfectly familiar—and
which was about an inch in length. I usually se
lected, for this purpose, a common pin. After i
little familiar conversation with them, about th
pin—of what it was made, etc.—I told them i
was an inch long ; and thus endeavored to fix i
their minds, as the starting point, a clear idea o
an inch. In the next place, I was accustomed t
show them other objects of the same real length
but whose apparent length is less, because the;
are thicker, or different in other respects. A grea
variety of objects was shown them, and great car
taken not to make a second step till the pupil ful
ly understood the first.

By placing two pins, or two other objects, eacl
an inch in length, in a line, I proceeded to sho;
them how great a distance two inches was, or thre
inches. But before I proceeded to repeat the incl
more than two or three times, I used to show then
my penknife, the handle of which constituted i
three inch rule, and required them to judge by th
eye, how long it was—that is, how many inches

It must be distinctly understood that I am her
speaking chiefly of exercises with little childrei
not yet advanced to geography. But it is quite obvi
ous to me, that the very same exercises were of

ten really needed by pupils ten, twelve, or fourteen years of age ; and that much of geography was wholly unmeaning to them for want of such instruction.

My little pupils were now prepared to judge—*guess* as I called it—of the length of other objects, especially other knives, pencils, combs, crayons, keys, etc. such as they were accustomed to see or have in their pockets. From objects three inches long, I proceeded, step by step, to those which were twelve inches in length. Here I paused, long enough to fix the idea pretty well ; after which I told them that twelve inches were a foot. From a foot, we proceeded slowly to a yard; which is as far as I ever went at a single lesson. I never proceeded as far as I might have done, however ; because I was always very cautious about continuing the exercises till I fatigued their minds, or disgusted them by my tediousness.

And now it was that I found their mental powers began to be active, when they read or heard about an inch, six inches, a foot, six or sixty feet. How long would six feet be ? they would ask themselves. And when they learned that a tall man was about six feet high, they were delighted to make that as a kind of measure. Thus if they read that a certain wild animal or tree was six feet and another twelve feet in height, they were

quite prepared to think of the one as of the height
of a man, and of the other as just about the height
of two men when the feet of one are placed upon
the head of the other.

They were also frequently asking their parents,
or brothers, or sisters, or other friends,—how long
is that ? or how many feet high is that ? or how
many inches long is that ?   It is surprizing how
these " keys" to knowledge will open and interest
and expand the minds of the young ; and prove
the means of gradually developing their intellectual powers.

But when from yards I went with them to rods,
they were still better pleased as well as better prepared to go forward in the study of geography.
It often happens that a certain piece of road, or
portion of a garden, with which a pupil is familiar,
is just three rods, or just four rods, or just six rods
wide.   Now when this is so, and a child comes to
fix this well in his mind, he uses it as a measure,
in forming an idea of distances of which he afterward hears or reads.   If he reads of a river which
is sixteen rods wide, and his father's garden which
at the end nearest the road is just four rods wide,
is his measure, he will naturally and easily form
an idea of the width of the stream by conceiving
of it as four times the width of the garden.

I do not say, indeed, that every child will in all

circumstances and in every case, make such comparisons, and draw such conclusions ; but an ingenious child who has been taught in the way above described, and who has also been properly taught in mental arithmetic, will be very apt to do so ; as I know from observation and experience. And I know, moreover, that without this preparatory knowledge, all our previous instruction in geography, involving as it does the mention of heights, distances, lengths, breadths, falls upon a child's ear like an unmeaning sound. Nor does it cease to do so, in every instance, when he ceases to be any longer a child. The habit is often continued through life. There are, indeed, very few people who when they peruse a book or newspaper which involves ideas of height or distance, perceive clearly, as soon as the language or figures are presented to the eye, and in its proper dimensions, the object. They slide over it. And this careless practice of sliding over things, is easily extended to the perusal of other words where no such difficulties present themselves : and indeed to everything else, which comes before the mind.

I ought to remark also, that every teacher or parent who pursues the course here indicated, with the child, should be very careful indeed to be accurate about distances ; and especially about all those distances which he is likely to adopt as measures. I know a man who when four or five years old was constantly told that a certain piece of road was a quarter of a mile long. This he made his measure ; so that when he thought of a mile he doubled this piece of road four times, in order to conceive of it. But it happened that his measure was about a fifth too long ; and hence his mile was a mile and one fifth. And one great evil is that though he now knows his error, yet to this day,—and he is nearly forty years old—he always, before he reflects upon it, refers his distances to his old measure.

The spirit of this species of elementary teaching I took great pains to infuse into my school during this whole season ; and I have reason to believe that by means of it a considerable amount of good was accomplished. Still, nothing was done in this way, in comparison with what should have been done. All our geography students in common schools—wise as they suppose themselves—ought, for at least six months, to go through with a species of this kind of drilling ; before they are fit to touch a geography.

SECTION IV.

A PRACTICAL EXERCISE.

Examples of it. Various modes of conducting it. Its advantages—novelty—in teaching spelling—defining —writing—reading—composition—geography — biography—history. Furnishes employment to the pupils. Cultivates all the mental faculties. Discovers their character. How it does this. Directions to teachers. Remarks on the spirit of Instruction.

This winter I introduced an exercise among my pupils, from which I found the most important advantages. I had indeed made some use of it in other schools, but never to any considerable extent. It consisted in incorporating—*framing*, as we called it—words into sentences.

I was in the habit of dictating, or giving out to my pupils,—each having his slate—a set of words, which they were required to write down. I always dictated very slowly, that all might have ample time. When the dictation was completed, they were required to exercise their ingenuity in so putting them into sentences of their own construction that they would make sense, as parts of those sentences.

Suppose the words dictated or given out were

apples, *corn*, *moon*, *hat*, *gold*, *red ;* and suppose the pupils were required to incorporate them into sentences. The following might be the result of the efforts of some very young pupils.

Apples are good to eat.   A new *hat*.
Corn grows.   *Gold* is yellow.
The bright *moon*.   A piece of *red* cloth.

Others would probably say much more. Perhaps their lists would read thus :

I am very fond of *apples*.   I love to look at the *moon*.
My father raises *corn*.   Some *hats* are made of wool.
Money is made of *gold* and silver and copper.
There is a bird called a *red* bird.

Sometimes I gave them a much longer list than this, and required them to select a certain number of the words, such as they chose, and " frame in.' I have sometimes given out twenty or thirty words and required them to select seven of those which appeared to them most interesting.

In other instances I have requested all those who preferred to do so, to select some favorite word and relate, on their slates, a story about it ; spending their whole time on that single word and the story. I have in this way occasionally drawn out quite a long story from a boy who at the first thought he could do nothing.

I recollect in particular, having given out, or

a certain occasion, the word *bee* among the rest. One of my boys, scarcely more than ten years of age, immediately wrote a long account of an adventure, in a meadow, with a nest of humble bees.

Another mode of this exercise, still more interesting to some of my older pupils, consisted in framing as many of the words of the list as they could into a single sentence or verse. I have sometimes found half a dozen or even more words crowded into two or three lines across the slate.

This exercise, in its varied forms and diversities, was one of the best I ever introduced into my school. It both interested my pupils, and was a source of much instruction. I have sometimes wondered that it is not oftener introduced into schools. Its advantages, among others, are the following:

It is *novel*. Children, it is well known, are always fond of something new. They soon get tired of their old school exercises, as they do of their old playthings. A new exercise, now and then, though it were in its own nature no better than the old, would, in reality, be more valuable; simply from its novelty.

It teaches *spelling*. The pupil, in writing down his words, is expected to spell them correctly. Indeed I sometimes made this a part of the exercise; either going round from scholar to scholar, and examining the slates, or requesting them to bring them to me for examination. In this way more real practical knowledge of spelling was probably acquired, in a lesson of six words, than is sometimes gained by a whole page of words arranged in columns and learned by rote.

It is a capital exercise in *defining.* This, indeed was one leading object. No child can practice in this way without making rapid progress in the knowledge and *use* of words, especially of the words designed for the exercise. And since we have few text books in defining, this is the best exercise I am acquainted with for a substitute.

It is a good exercise in *writing.* I have known children become tolerable writers merely by writing on their slates. In any event, this exercise cannot fail to be of advantage in this respect.

It may furnish a *reading* lesson. It was customary with me to require my pupils to *read* their sentences, when thus framed. One great difficulty—perhaps the greatest—in teaching the young to read, is, that they do not enter into the spirit of the author's intention. Even when they appear to understand him, they fall much short of his meaning. But this difficulty is obviated when they form their own lessons. It cannot be otherwise than that they understand them. They must enter into their spirit. But if so, they can read them properly.

How often have I been told by my teachers—
ow often have I told my own pupils the same
ing—that the great rule in reading is to read as
e talk. But it is next to impossible to read the
nguage of others as we would talk it; because,
ter all, it is not our *own* language, it is that of
other. Here, the language, as I have already
served, is the pupil's own; and it is not so diffi-
lt for him to read it as he would talk it. Ined most pupils will be apt to do so, so far as I
ve observed. Mine certainly were.

It is a valuable exercise in *composition.* No
here, perhaps, do the majority of teachers mis-
ke more than in teaching the art of composition.
hey seem often to expect the pupil, to have
oughts on subjects which are wholly beyond his
pacity. Hence it is that they are required to
rite on abstract subjects; as 'Good manners,'
rly rising, beauty, riches, and the like. And
nce it is, too, that the pupils so often dread the
sk.

I never knew a child that might not be led into
e habit of composing with the utmost ease, pro-
ded he commenced right. Indeed, so far are they
om having a dread of the exercise, I believe most
the young, with suitable management and en-
uragement, would be very fond of it.

In the case which has led to these remarks, I

almost always found my pupils pleased with the idea of writing something of their own ; although they were not always, it is true, equally pleased to exhibit it to the whole school : nor was this insisted on. How they would have regarded the exercise had I told them that one principal object I had in view, in requiring it, was to teach them composition, I do not know ; perhaps I should have frightened them by a name which, by some means or other is to the young almost odious.

It may be made an exercise in *geography*. We have only to give out suitable words as Boston China, or Madeira, and encourage them to tell us all they know or can learn about these places ; and it then becomes in effect, a lesson—often a very useful one—in this most interesting branch.

The same is true of several other things. By giving the names of distinguished men or women as Alfred, Alexander, Howard, Newell, etc ; or curious beasts, birds, or fishes ; and of plants minerals etc. you may at the same time be doing something in the departments of history or biography, or in those of botany, mineralogy and the other branches of natural science. At least, the exercise will have a bearing upon the various sciences I have named ; and will tend to furnish the keys to it.

There are several other important advantages

esulting from this exercise. One is that it may
e used in school to fill up any otherwise vacant
moments. Such moments sometimes do occur.
hildren, for the time, seem to have little to do,
nd are either dispirited or inclined to go to play.
a this, or any other emergency, you can easily
rrest their attention, and furnish them with plea-
ng and at the same time useful employment.
o do this, all of them must, it is true, have slates;
at I consider a slate as necessary to every pupil
a the school, as a spelling book, and much more
>; and during several of the latter years of
y teaching, if parents would not furnish each
upil with a slate and pencil, I bought and loaned
em to him.

Another advantage is that it improves in a most
armonious and happy manner, all the faculties
the mind. Memory is not in this case, as it too
ommonly is in school, exclusively cultivated;
ey are required to reflect, compare and judge.
specially does it improve the faculty of judging.
his is perhaps its highest recommendation.

Lastly, it developes, in a most wonderful man-
er, the peculiar habits and tastes of each individ-
il. We hear much said—and justly too—of
e importance of having an instructor understand
lly the character of his pupils. Now I know of
thing that will accomplish this object so well as

the foregoing exercise. It discovers, at once, th leading propensities or characteristic traits of eac pupil—I mean if you introduce and manage th exercise properly ; otherwise you may defeat th whole intention of it.

If it be asked *how* this exercise discovers, a remarkably, the character of the child, I reply by showing on what topics his thoughts dwell wit most pleasure. It is curious indeed to see in wha manner pupils will select from a list, say of fift words, embracing every variety. Some will a ways select names of qualities or properties, a sweet, green, or hot. Others always select name of number or quantity or amount, as thousand pound, etc. Others will select topics still differ ent. But their leading traits of character will b still better known by the manner in which the treat their various topics. Boys of an enterpri ing or aspiring character will not only choose th name of some distinguished warrior or travelle but recount more or less of his " glorious" deed Others, who are benevolently inclined, thoug they select even the same name, will relate h deeds of benevolence. Others, still, trained to th love of money or the gratification of their app tites, are very apt to drag into their little stori something that savors of rich eating or drinl ing, or of property.

Since I have spoken of conducting this exercise in a proper manner, it is necessary to add that I would always endeavor so to manage it as to have the pupils regard it as a favor ; and not as a task. To this end it must not be too long continued, especially at first. It is always better to leave off a little earlier rather than not return to the same fare with a good appetite. Nor is it well to be too critical at first, especially with the exertions of the timid or diffident. By over, or rough criticism, I have sometimes so far discouraged beginners in this exercise, that they never completely recovered from the injury.

Indeed, all exercises in school, of whatever nature they may be, require, in the teacher, a large fund of plain good sense. No male or female teacher can take up any plan or method whatever from another person, and introduce it into school, and render it permanently useful, without certain modifications, or restrictions, to adapt it to the peculiar circumstances of themselves. There is no method of teaching any branch in the world which will always apply to the circumstances of all schools. It has been said that a coat properly cut and made will fit any body. But if this is obviously untrue, how much more untrue is it that particular plans and methods of teaching are adapted to all schools ?—For myself, I have no doubt that the

exercise which I have here described, and which
I deem a highly important one, would be of exceed
ing great value, in at least *some* of its features, t
all teachers who would enter fully into its spirit
Here is one great secret of many methods of in
struction. It is not the improved method itsel
which does the good, so much as the spirit of hin
who adopts it. And where a teacher has a prope
spirit, and is truly spirited, he may accomplish a
great deal by methods in themselves quite inferio
as well as by antiquated or inferior school book
and plans for discipline.

SECTION V.

EXPERIMENT IN TEACHING ETYMOLOGY.

Preparation. Sensible objects. Teaching the Noun
The Verb. The Pronoun. Meeting in the morning
at sunrise. Adjectives. Adverbs. Mood and tense
etc. Results of the experiment. Reflections.

I was resolved on making an experiment i
teaching English Grammar. It was perfectly ob
vious that as Etymology was usually taught i
schools, it was not only not understood by pupils
but irksome, in the extreme. I thought I had a

ast devised a plan of inculcating this part of grammar with more than usual success, as well as in a manner which would be agreeable to the pupils.

These points being settled, the question was, when and where to make the experiment. Its novelty would so attract the attention of the rest of the scholars, if it was pursued in the regular hours of the day school, as to render that season somewhat doubtful. Besides, there were such prejudices in the district—and in most other school districts in that region—against grammar in general, that I was afraid to render it very conspicuous, lest I should displease the parents.

Our evenings remained ; but I was, in general, opposed to evening schools. The evening, however, presenting fewest objections, it was concluded to pursue the course, at those seasons. We commenced the evening of the first day of January, 1830.

As I had given some intimations of my plan to the pupils, I had expected a large class would attend the course. But the inclemency of the weather, just at the time when we made the beginning, together with other unfavorable circumstances, diminished the class to about ten ; of whom, there were about an equal number of males and females. Their ages were generally from twelve to sixteen years ; though there were a few not much over ten.

Each pupil was furnished with slate, pencil an
sponge, and each was required to pay the close
possible attention to everything I said or did.   Th
idea of studying grammar with slates and pencil
was so novel, that I found no difficulty of secur
ing general attention.

Holding up my cane before them, I asked ther
to write the name of it on their slates.   It wa
immediately and eagerly done.   Some, indeed
wrote *staff*, instead of cane ; but this was a ma
ter of no consequence.   Either was sufficient fc
the purpose.

Now, said I, after giving them all ample tin
to write the first word, you may write the name
that, placing my hand upon the table : which we
accordingly done.   I had already requested the
to be careful to spell correctly, as well as to wri
everything in a legible hand.

You may now, I observed, write down on yo
slates the names of all the things in the schoc
room : such as chairs, desks, windows, etc.   Or
of the pupils at first observed, that there were b
few things in the room.   But he soon found, (
observing more closely and thinking more intens
ly, that the number was much greater than he ha
previously supposed.   There were more than I
found room for on the whole of one side of I
slate.   Many of the class said they could not, b

ore now, have believed there were so many things
n the room.

When each had extended his list as far as he
could, I requested him to count them, and set
down the number. Particular individuals were
next called upon to read their list aloud, pronouncing distinctly each letter. When there was an
error in orthography, it was marked, to be afterwards corrected.

As soon as this exercise was finished, and the
slates cleaned, I asked them to put down the names
of all the objects they could think of, which they
were accustomed to see in the road between the
school house and Mr. B.'s—about a quarter of a
mile distant. One pupil inquired, if they might
write the names of the men, and women, and children, he was accustomed to see there ; as well as
the birds, snakes, and other animals. I told him
that he might.

A long list having been completed by each pupil, he was required to read it, mark the errors in
orthography, and correct them as before. Care
was taken not to make the lesson tedious. It was
not expected they would, at these first efforts, succeed in writing down every name, that might have
occurred to me. All we wanted, was to make a
beginning.

As they were not yet fatigued at all, I gave

them a third lesson. Do you know what a quadruped is ! I said. Either they did not know, or did not understand me, for they were silent. I told them that quadruped simply meant an animal with four legs. Now, said I, you may write down the names of all the animals you have seen, read or heard of with four legs. A long list was soon produced and corrected as before.

Josiah, said I, do you know what a quadruped is? An animal which has four legs, he replied. I gave examples of a few bipeds and quadrupeds; and asked him to distinguish the latter. He found no difficulty in doing so.

It was scarcely an hour from the time of our commencing the lesson; and yet they were all eager to do more. So I gave them short lessons on the names of flowers—trees—fishes—trades—articles of furniture, etc.

Before closing the exercises for the evening, we reviewed what we had done, in a very familiar manner: I, on my part, asking them what we had done, at every step of our progress; and they, on their part, giving the particulars.

Now, I said to them, you have many of you attended schools where grammar was studied; do you know what a noun is? No one appeared able to tell. They had heard the language of the definitions of the book repeated over and over—

erhaps repeated it themselves—but had not un-
erstood it ; and now, they had utterly forgotten it.

Well, said I, all the words which you have writ-
en on your slates this evening are nouns.   They
re *names* of things ; and all names are nouns.
Noun, then, means *name*.   You may wonder why
ve do not always call them names instead of us-
ng the word noun ; but I can only tell you at
reseut, that the word noun, in studying grammar,
s the most fashionable.

You must, however, be aware that you have
vritten the names of only a small part of the things
n the world.   There are names of good conduct,
nd bad conduct, and there are names of a great
nany sorts of things which you do not probably
hink of.

If a man should behave so ill, as to take things
vithout liberty, and perhaps do it a great many
imes, there would be a name for him ; do you
now what it would be ?   They did not quite un-
lerstand me at first, but afterwards they did ; and
aid *a thief*.   I gave other familiar examples of
iouns ; and for variety's sake, as well as to en-
orce the principle, asked them to turn to a cer-
ain table of words in their spelling books, and
elect all of those words which they thought were
iouns.

We had now continued the exercise an hour

and a half, when it was deemed advisable to clos
for the evening. There was no diminution of in
terest, however, till we came to the very momen
of dismission.

At our next meeting, it was my object to giv
them a clear and distinct idea of a verb. I di
not, it is true, tell them beforehand that we wer
going to study the verb; for it was a part of my
plan not to do it. I only requested them to tak
their seats, and to provide themselves as before
with slates and pencils.

I had entered the room with a bough in my
hand, which I had broken from a tree, by the road
side, as I came along. The scholars had stare
as I came in, but had not probably supposed
had anything to do with the lesson. They wer
soon undeceived, however. The bough was t
be, for that evening, my text book.

Observe now, said I, what I do, and write dow
the action which you see me perform. This di
tinction they did not at first fully comprehenc
Accordingly, I broke in two a portion of the bough
and asked what it was I had done. *Broke* th
stick, said one. Well, then, said I, if broke is th
word which you think will best describe what
have just been doing, write it down. It was ac
cordingly done; and I could now perceive tha
they began to understand me.

Taking my penknife from my pocket, I next cut the stick, having already required them to watch my movements. This action they were now required to write down. They found no difficulty in doing it. Some, indeed, wrote the nominative along with the verb, as ' *he* cut' or ' he cuts ;' but in general they wrote only the verb, in some of its moods or tenses.

A very great number of actions were now performed on or with the stick ;—it was split, hacked, scraped, bent, swung, tossed, sawed, peeled, etc. All these words, and many more, were written on their slates. Other actions were then performed and disposed of in the same manner; such as stamping, leaping, jumping, walking, crouching, running, sitting, rising, singing, whistling, whispering, frowning, smiling, etc.

When these exercises had been continued an hour or more, I told them that there was a name for words that meant action ; and that the name was *verb*. Thus, said I, you have the true meaning of the word verb; it signifies an action. It is a meaning, too, which you will never forget. When we learn in the book that ' a verb is a word which signifies to be, to do, or to suffer,' we seldom understand it ; and when it is explained to us, we are apt to forget it. But you will now remember what a verb is as long as you live. -True,

I have not told you everything I know about the verb ; but all that I have told you is true, and may be easily remembered. I repeat it, I do not think you can *easily* forget it.

And I do not believe they have forgotten it to this hour ; though more than seven years have elapsed. It is the only true mode of teaching the definitions of those parts of speech ; and the principle is applicable not only to etymology, but to orthography, as well as to several sciences quite distinct from English grammar.

Our exercise was finished, for this evening, by selecting all the verbs in certain columns of words to which I referred them, and by a review, both of the studies of this and the previous evening.

I have been thus particular in describing my method of teaching the character of the verb and noun, because, in the first place, I wish to illustrate the general principle of teaching the thing itself, before I meddled with its name ; and in the second place, because the noun and verb, as is well known, are really two very important parts of speech ; and require, on their own account, a large share of the learner's early attention. He who gets a clear idea of the true nature of the noun and the verb, and can select them all from the page of an English book, with scarcely a single mistake has made a very considerable step toward a correct knowledge of English grammar.

At our next lesson we studied the pronoun.
For this purpose, I selected a familiar story, with
which they were all acquainted, and which aboun-
ded with pronouns, especially *he;* and requested
hem to write the story on their slates, exactly as
should slowly repeat it to them. In repeating
t, I substituted nouns for the pronouns, in every
nstance, which in some places made a complete
argon of it. They were then requested to erase
he nouns, as many of them as they could, and
ubstitute words which would make better sense
n their place. As soon as I had made myself-
ntelligible by an example or two, they proceeded
n the work with great pleasure and interest.

When several similar exercises had been per-
ormed, they were told that those words which
hey put in the place of nouns, and which had so
much abridged and improved the composition,
vere *pronouns.* *Pro,* I said, is a Latin word, and
neans *for.* *Pro-noun* therefore means *for a noun;*
hat is, a substitute for a noun.

During this evening, we confined ourselves en-
irely to the personal pronoun, and to a review of
his and the preceding lessons, and to selecting
nouns, verbs, and pronouns from some of the ta-
les of the spelling book.

Such was the eagerness of my pupils to advance
with the experiment that we had our fourth lesson

in the morning at sunrise ; and this, too, in spite
of the intense cold, and in defiance of the fact tha
several of the pupils were females, and had near
ly a mile to walk to reach the school house.

At this morning meeting, we did nothing bu
study the nature of number—singular and plura
I must not go into details of the plan for want c
room. It is sufficient to say that the plan wa
equally well adapted to the purpose, with thos
which had been devised for other purposes at ou
former meetings ; that we spent some time at thi
as at every lesson, in reviewing the past ; and the
we closed only when we were interrupted by th
arrival of the hour of nine o'clock ; the signal fc
commencing the regular forenoon exercises.

Our time, at the fifth meeting, was taken u
with the adjective ; in reviewing former lesson
and selecting nouns, verbs, etc. from spelling an
reading lessons ; or in *parsing*, as I should sa
etymologically. I will not describe the plan ;
will only say, that the principle and the end wes
similar to those of former lessons, and that th
pupils' interest was undiminished.

The sixth lesson was on the gender of nou
and pronouns. The seventh was a review of a
we had done ; at which I was agreeably surpris
to find that though two or three weeks had elaps
since the exercises were commenced, not a sing

23

dea had been lost by the most careless scholar. I attributed this—no doubt justly—in part to the inerest which was taken, and not wholly to the original excellence of the method.

The eighth lesson was intended to show the relaion of adjectives to nouns; and was therefore partly an exercise of syntax. The real object, however, was to show the true nature and character of the adjective, by exhibiting its connection in the sentences where it occurs. We also took up, in this lesson, the degrees of comparison.

The ninth lesson was on the adverb, but I need not go into detail. I have extended the subject too much already.

It is just necessary to say that we closed with our tenth lesson. This was spent on mood and tense. Want of time—but not the want of success, prevented a further prosecution of the experiment. We had, however, proceeded far enough to convince me that there is nothing in the nature of grammar itself, were it pursued in a rational manner, to excite or preserve the disgust for it which children are so apt to acquire.

For though we had not spent more than twentyfour hours of time in our experiment—even including the time occupied in studying three or four short lists of words at home, connected with our course—yet in this very short period, a considerable advance had been made, not in study of Grammar itself as a whole, but in the important department of it called etymology. The pupils had acquired a thorough understanding of the nature of the adjective and of the degrees of comparison ; of the nature of nouns, with gender and number, and partially, case ; of personal pronouns ; and of verbs in general, and adverbs. They had also acquired some knowledge of transitive and intransitive verbs ; of mood and tense ; of government and agreement ; and of the nature of prepositions, conjunctions, interjections and articles ; they could parse, etymologically, as well as scholars in general, who have studied grammar three months on the common plan ; and what they had gone over with, they clearly understood.

Enough at least had been accomplished—I repeat the sentiment—to convince me, along with another experiment somewhat similar to this, that if English Grammar must be studied by young children, there is a better mode than requiring them to spend weeks and months in committing to memory and repeating definitions and rules, to which they do not and cannot possibly attach any meaning.

Not that books are to be dispensed with, altogether ; far enough from that. Where some preparatory knowledge has been acquired, books are

nost unquestionably, highly useful ; nay, indisensable.   But in the etymological part of the
study, the pupil's own eyes and mind, with his
slate and pencil, constitute the best books ; and
without these, to begin with, the use of books, is,
o young children, of very little service.

What sort of an impression was produced on
he minds of the people of the district by this experiment, I never knew.   I had reason to believe
however that they regarded it as the visionary
plan and ultimate failure of one who was prone to
speculation and innovation.   There were indeed
some circumstances calculated to give rise to the
opinion that I was inclined to speculation.   I had
at this period some very curious and to them vis-
onary ethical opinions, which I was sure of vent-
ng, whenever and wherever I could get any body
o hear me.   It was not therefore singular that I
should be misunderstood in an experiment in ety-
nology which was so exceedingly novel, and so
unlike anything of which they had before heard.

SECTION VI.

TEACHING ORTHOGRAPHY.

Partial experiment. Examples. Various kinds of or
thographical parsing. Great saving of time by teach
ing orthography in this manner.

The new method of teaching Etymology gradu
ally suggested to my mind the idea of teaching
orthography in the same manner; also the nature
of accent, emphasis, etc.; instead of going through
that long—*long*—process so common in our schools
but which is seldom so far understood and made
practical as to render it of much service. I has
tened to put the plan in execution; but circum
stances prevented my carrying the experimen
far enough, to test with certainty, its merits.

No committing to memory, in the usual and
popular sense of the phrase, is required. The
teacher requests his pupils to take their spelling
books—any other book would answer just as wel
—and open to a certain place which he designates
and hold themselves in readiness to answer such
questions as he may propose. The following wil
exhibit the spirit of the process.

The teacher requests the class to observe, on
the right hand page, the word *baker*; and on the
left hand page, the word *name*, and compare them

23*

Are they alike ? says he. "No." In what do hey differ ? "The word *baker* is the longest, and has the most letters in it." Is that all the difference ? "No ; the word *baker* is divided." How divided ? "Into two parts." You mean two syllables. It is so. *Baker* has two syllables, while *name* has but one. *Ba* is the first syllable, and *ker* the second.

Now turn over the four next leaves on your right hand, and tell me how many syllables there are in the last word on the right hand page. "There are four." Very well ; you may now answer my questions without referring to the book. How many syllables are there in the word *behave* ? "Two." How many in *atonement* ? "Three." Great Britain ? "Three." Ice ? "One." *Impenetrability* ? "Seven."

Do you know of any name by which all words of only one syllable are sometimes called ? "No." I will direct you to a place where you can find out. Please to turn to such a page, (designating the page) you may read that sentence, (pointing to it.) "A word of one syllable is called a monosyllable." Very well. Endeavor to find out now, what a word of two syllables is called. When you find out, you may read, or repeat it. "A word of two syllables is called a dissyllable."—Now think, if you can, of some word which is a dissyllable, and tell me when you have thought "Table ; pencil ; inkstand ; window." That is sufficient.

The same slow and gradual but natural course is pursued till the pupil thoroughly understands what a syllable is, that though he may not be able to repeat the language of the book, he can at all times, tell you what a monosyllable is,—a dissyllable,—a trissyllable—etc. The process, thus far if examples enough are cited to render the whole sufficiently intelligible, may take up the time o two short lessons.

It will next be proper to analyze syllables. A word of one syllable is first selected ;—say *at* You see, says the teacher, that there are two let ters in this little monosyllable. Are they precisely alike ? "No." How do they differ ? "One i *a* and the other is *t.*" True ; but there is anothe difference, which I am now about to explain. will direct to a sentence—you may read it. "Th vowels are *a, e, i, o, u,* and sometimes *w,* and *y.*' You see then that some of the letters of the alpha bet are called vowels, do you not ? "Yes." Now tell me whether any of the letters in the word *a* belong to this number. "Yes, *a.*" Does not *t* "No." Is not *t* then a vowel ? "No."

Other monosyllables, including other vowels are treated in the same manner. It is unnecessary at first, to speak of the consonants, except to say that they are not vowels; but we should confine ourselves, as much as possible, to one thing at a time; and first teach that thoroughly. *W* and *y* may also, at first, be omitted. But as soon as the vowels are readily distinguished from the consonants, the teacher proceeds.

Here is the word *amber.* Is it a monosyllable? " No." What then? " A dissyllable." What is *a*, a vowel or a consonant? " A vowel." What is *m*? What is *b*? What is *e*? What is *r*?

When this exercise has been pursued till the whole class can distinguish every vowel and every consonant—but not in my opinion before—it may be well to explain the nature of the vowels and consonants respectively. I begin with the consonants.

Suppose we take up the word *magic.* Is this a monosyllable, or a dissyllable? " A dissyllable." Is *m* a vowel or a consonant? " A consonant." Here after referring the class to the two kinds of consonants, mutes and semi-vowels, I inquire; Is *m* a mute or a semi-vowel? " I do not know." But examine your list of mutes. Do you not find it there? " No." Is it among the semi-vowels? " Yes."

What is *a*? " A vowel." What is *g*? " A consonant." Has it here the hard or soft sound?

" The soft." Is it then a mute, or a semi-vowel ?
" A semi-vowel." What is *i?* What is *c?* Is
it a mute or a semi-vowel ?

When everything is understood, thus far, the
various sounds of the vowel *a* are introduced ;
afterward those of *e ;* and subsequently the rest,
one at a time. When these are familiar, the diphthongs and triphthongs are attended to, then the
compound characters, not only those which represent simple sounds, but others ; and finally, the
silent letters.

The same principles will guide us in teaching
the nature of accent, emphasis and cadence ; of
primitive, derivative, and compound words ; and
the art of designating the vowel sounds, in the tables, by figures. It is not, however, sufficient for
the learner to understand, merely, what figure
governs the sound of the principal vowel, in the
accented syllable ; he must also be able to state
what figure *would* be placed over every vowel in
a word, in order to mark its true sound.

When this whole subject has been gradually
developed and presented to the mind of a child,
the questions, during an exercise, might be something like the following ;—the word selected for
the purpose being *rhinoceros.*

Which is the accented syllable of the word *rhinoceros?* What figure should be placed over it,

to mark the sound correctly? Has *o* any other sounds?. What figures would indicate each of them? Are there any other vowels in the word? Name one. What figure would govern that, if we were to place a figure over it? How many other sounds has *i*, and what figures would mark them? A similar course may be pursued with regard to *e*.

Is *r* a vowel, or a consonant? a mute or a semivowel? Is it ever silent? Has it more than one sound?—What is *h*? Is it ever silent? How is it in this instance?—Is *n* a consonant? a mute or a semi-vowel? Is it ever silent? Has it more than one sound?—What is *c*? Has it more than one sound? Which sound has it here? Is it then, a mute or a semi-vowel? (We may omit *r*, as it has occurred in the first syllable of the word). What is *s*, a mute or a semi-vowel? Has it ever more than one sound? Which has it in the present instance?

If we were to select for parsing—for this is none other than the true method of orthographical parsing—the word *thousand* or *champaign*, questions would naturally arise on the diphthongs *ou* and *ai*; and on the sounds of the compound characters *ch* and *th*; and on the silent *g*, etc.

From the knowledge I have of the common methods of teaching these things; from the partial experiments I have made, in this method ; and from the very nature of the case, I am confident that thirty minutes a day, spent in this way, with a class for three months, will give them a more thorough knowledge of the subject than ten, yes, twenty times that amount of time spent as it usually has been—and to some extent still is—in our common schools, especially in New England.

SECTION VII.

FORCING KNOWLEDGE.

An Error. Its effects real and imaginary. Jealousy. Never having time enough. Relating stories in school. Irritability.

One error still ran through all my movements in school, and proved a perpetual drawback upon my efforts. My anxiety led me to try to force knowledge upon my pupils. Not that I intended any forcing process, for I knew better. Still there was a feeling of haste, in all that I was doing ; a sort of opinion that we did not get along so fast or accomplish so much, or do it so well as we ought. I was never satisfied with myself when I reflected at all ; and I was little better satisfied with those around me.

This state of mind led me into many imaginary difficulties, as well as into a few real ones. Among other things it made me constantly suspicious that somebody would speak lightly of the school. Now there can be no surer way than this to bring about the very result which is so much dreaded. Strange that men with professedly wise heads, should be so prone to this error as some of us are !

But it also led me into the difficulty of never having time enough for our exercises. I was almost always deluged with work. I seldom had less than twice as much to do as really ought to have been done in the time. Besides, it led me to continue the school beyond the customary hours ; and to shorten the intermission and the periods of recess. It so absorbed all our time, in school, that it left me none, or at least next to none, for explanations, illustrations, relating of stories, etc. And yet these are the very things which by the interest they impart, and the impression they leave on the mind, constitute all, or nearly all, that is worth having, in a common district school. There is—there can be—no greater mistake than to suppose that nothing is done in school, unless you can count it in pages—pages spelled, read, recited, written, etc. And yet it is the very mistake which I was constantly making ; and which greatly tended, directly and indirectly, to all my other errors, and the consequent misery which attended them.

I spoke of relating stories to my pupils. Now I may be a little singular in this respect; but it does seem to me that a "knack" at story telling is one of the most important qualifications in a school master, next to good moral and religious principles and a correct example, which can be named. An occasional story, well told, is not only a refreshment and a relief, to the bodies and minds of the pupils; but if it be of the right kind, may have a very excellent effect on the heart. A writer in the Annals of Education thinks that every college should have in it a Professor of story telling. Now I am sure that a good story teller is at least as necessary in a common school, as in a college.—But it will be of no use to have the art of story telling, if a teacher so manages that he never finds time to use it.

My desire for making haste to have my pupils learned,—in other words my attempts to force knowledge upon them—thwarted as my hopes and endeavors seemed constantly to be—resulted in a kind of disappointment whose pangs were constantly rending me and leaving me miserable; especially in the school room. But of all places in the world, the school room is the last in which

24

we ought to feel ourselves miserable. There, if any where, we should feel well ; and manifest our good feelings in our every feature. There if any where, it is our duty—yes, our *duty*—to be, if possible, blessed, and happy.

SECTION VIII.

TEACHING PUPILS TO SIT STILL.

" Sitting still." The School room not a prison. Advantages of learning to sit still. Example of a want of this habit. How formed. Four objections to sitting still too long at once. The golden mean. Constant employment.

In my early teaching, I was very fond of the pleasure, and I may say the reputation too, of having my pupils *sit still* in school. But such silence as I then desired, as I have already said elsewhere, is procured at too great an expense. Subsequent experience has taught me that, except for a few minutes at a time, on certain occasions, children should not be thus dealt with. They should not feel that they are in a *prison*, but in a *school*.

The attempt to make young children, at our district schools, sit still unemployed, for an hour at a time, has often struck me as not only unwise

—since it is usually fruitless—but unreasonable

Such protracted stillness has no advantages' to compensate for the trouble of securing it ; besides, it is next to impossible to effect it.

The only advantages that I have heard claimed for it, are that it is important to the child in future life to have learned to sit still ; and that it is equally important to the good order of the school.

I admit, with cheerfulness, the importance to the child himself, of learning to sit still. I consider scarcely anything which is taught, either in the family or in the school, of more consequence. For the want of such knowledge—for want of the *habit*, I should rather say, of sitting still—I have seen even adults unhappy.

One man, in particular, I recollect, who was never taught to sit still. He is now forty years of age. Follow him where you will, even to the church ; and unless he is asleep, you will find him in motion. I have, indeed, known him to make efforts to keep still ; but they are never long continued. If he can do nothing else, he will pick his teeth or his finger nails. He perceives his condition, and makes some faint efforts to break from the chains of so powerful a habit ; but he finds it so difficult, that he does not long persevere in his attempts.

But how is this habit to be formed ? Is it to be

formed, in the boy or girl of three or four or five years of age, by compelling him or her to sit, with arms folded, on an unpleasant or painful seat an hour at a time? Never. Such is the nature of most children, that unless you fasten them, or employ them, you cannot keep them still so long, if you would. The time for which a child should be taught to sit perfectly still, either in school or elsewhere, should be, at first, very short indeed; and should only be increased gradually. The moment you extend the period, too much, you not only defeat your object, for the time, but you produce, in the child's mind, a permanent reaction or dislike to the whole thing.

In regard to the plea that a little child ought to sit still, for the good of the rest of the school, I have many doubts. The older pupils are not much influenced by the example of the younger class of whom I am just now speaking. The force of example, in a school, is all the other way. If examples of perfect silence were even as valuable in a school, as some suppose, it should be the older, and not the younger pupils, of whom they they should be required.

But I have not found this deathlike silence in a school room either useful or necessary. True, I have sometimes required it of my pupils. But at other times, I have permitted more of the hum of business. If there were a difference at all in the results, I think the last mentioned course the best.

In this view, it seems to me wrong to impose on young children so painful a task as that of sitting entirely still for a whole hour at a time. It seems not only irrational, but as I have already said, unreasonable. It not only has no important advantages, but it is attended with many positive evils.

1. It is injurious to health. No child under five years of age ought to be expected to sit still half an hour at a time, in any circumstances. Who can doubt that the spine is often injured in this way ? Who can doubt, that the universal or almost universal crookedness of this naturally straight column, is often begun in the school room, in sitting too long on hard benches, and above all, in sitting too still ? What other young animal— except the human being—would not be destroyed in a short time, by such treatment ? And do not young children suffer quite as much from close confinement, as other young animals ? Is not motion, almost incessantly, as indispensable to the proper and healthy developement of the organs and frame of the human body, as to those of the lamb, or the kitten, or the kid ?

2. It endangers good manners and habits. A thousand bad habits—physical, intellectual and moral—grow out of the effort to keep little child-

ren still in the school room. There seems such a tendency to expend voluntary power in some direction or another, that if they are required not to move their bodies, they will at least move their hands and feet. Hence, frequently arise the habits of drumming with the toes, rubbing the eyes, and picking the teeth, nose and ears. Hence, also arises, in some instances, the habit of picking or biting off the nails. I have seen those, in whom this last habit was rendered so inveterate at school, that they had not broken it up in middle age.

3. It is dangerous to morals. Children can no more bear to be idle, than adults; and it is at least equally true of them, that he who is idle, is sure to be in mischief. The seeds of a great multitude of vicious habits are sown while sitting on the school bench, with nothing to do.

4. It is a great waste of time to the teacher, if not to the pupil. What teacher has not regretted the necessity of spending so much of his time in correcting and punishing his pupils? Yet no small portion of this correction and punishment grow out of idleness, aided by fruitless efforts to keep them perfectly still. How much happier would everybody be who is concerned—pupil, teacher and parent—if means were devised to keep these young folks constantly occupied! But

is it an impossibility to do so? Are there no means of furnishing the youngest pupil with such constant employment as to prevent the evils which it often costs both him and ourselves great pains to correct?

Yes, the means are abundant. There is no sort of difficulty—were teachers awake to the necessities of the case—of devising means for keeping every child in school in such constant employ as to prevent all the evils which are usually attendant upon idleness. Let his time be properly divided between business and play and sitting, and the task is accomplished.

Suppose a class of little boys have been sitting a quarter of an hour in perfect silence. This is quite as long a time as any body should expect them to be still. Then give each of them a slate and pencil, fifteen minutes more. Let them write down the lessons they are learning; or make pictures; or do anything almost, they please. Then perhaps, let them recite, or spell, or say their letters. Then let them go out and play fifteen minutes more. Then, again, you may require them to sit perfectly still a short time. Then, slates again. Then, it may be well to let them stand a short time; and so on.

Let me say again, there is no sort of difficulty in all this; especially if the school is not too large.

I have found no difficulty in carrying out the leading features of this plan in a school of forty pupils. If the number is very great, the teacher may be obliged to employ monitors to attend to the slate exercises, as well as to attend them during their recreations out of doors.

SECTION IX.

MY MORAL INFLUENCE.

Example more powerful than precept. Anecdote of tying shoes. An excellent lesson to me. Other examples of failure in teachers—in others. Necessity of attention to this subject. General effects of my own example in school. A gross failure. The Sunday evening club.

It had long been with me an established principle, that example, in a school master, was more powerful than precept. Not that it is not so in every body else ; but if there be a class of men, to whom the principle is especially applicable, and of especial importance, it is the teacher ; and next to him, perhaps, the parent.

In my early career as a pedagogue, I recollect having had one lively little pupil, who when so closely watched that he could not play with any

one near him, nor do anything else to reliev
himself from the *tedium* of his situation, woul
employ himself in tying and untying his shoe
At last I forbade this! But nature was too stron
for him ; he was soon at it again ; and as the cor
sequence—it was in my days of error on this sul
ject—he had his ears boxed !

Not long afterward, I think it was the very ne
day—I found myself tying one of my own shoe
in the school room, and in full sight of the boy
How many times I had done it before, during th
winter, and thus contradicted by example, what
taught by precept and endeavored to enforce b
punishment, I do not know. But the thought c
my inconsistency and unreasonableness cam
upon me now, like a shock of electricity. I won
dered at my folly, and firmly resolved to say n
more to the boy till I had first reformed myself.

This was a most excellent lesson ; and led m
to watch over my own conduct with a severer scru
tiny than I had ever done before. In the matte
of tying shoestrings, I believe I was never caugh
any more ; but I often detected myself in trans
gressing my own laws, in other matters. The
scholars were forbidden to gaze at people throug
the windows, as they passed by ; but I found my
self doing it, in one instance. But here, too,
broke up the practice at once.

This subject, I am led to think, is one of far greater importance than the bulk of our teachers suppose. Indeed I have met with many who never appeared to regard it at all. They made good and salutary laws for the pupils ; but as for themselves, they did not hesitate to violate them—at least in spirit—half a dozen times a day.

But why will they do this ? Why will they expect their precepts to be duly heeded, while their own example continues so bad ? Why will they not learn to be what they wish their pupils to be ?

It is easy to see the force of example, in a school master. One man I well remember, whose mild tones and mildness of manner wrought so—for he was universally beloved—upon his pupils, as to soften the manners and tones, and indeed the whole aspect of the rudest boys in school. I have even seen horses and cattle wrought upon, and affected in the same way by a master whose tones of voice were mild and gentle.

The truth is, that teachers in general, do not come up, in this respect, to the dignity of their profession ; and some fall wofully short of it. These things ought not so to be. They must not be so. They must change their course. They must strive to be, in all things to which the acutest young immortal mind can penetrate, exactly what they would have—would wish—their pupils to be.

It was now more than twelve years since I ha
been more or less engaged as a teacher ; and ye
it was not until now that I had fully considere
this whole subject of example. Nor do I know
that I should have considered it well till this ver
time, had it not been for the circumstance of th
shoe strings. This opened my eyes, and led m
to reflection. So much do we owe, many time
to very small events, and sometimes, even to ou
own blunders.

When parents and teachers shall fully under
stand, and duly consider the subject of exampl
in all its force, and under all its bearings—whe
they shall not only understand and consider it, bu
in all things govern themselves accordingly—whe
they shall come to act up to the true dignity o
parents and teachers, and set in all respects, sucl
an example as becomes them—then, perhaps no
till then, may we hope for an entire revolution ii
the affairs of our moral and religious—yes, an
our political world.

I have spoken as if I had learned, by this time
how to teach well by example ; and as if I acted
according to my knowledge. In some respect
truly, I did so, but in others I failed altogether.
sometimes looked anxious and care worn. A
others, I was melancholy and apprehensive. A
others, still, I was jealous and suspicious. And in

some instances, too, and these I have reason to fear, not few, my countenance showed the most certain marks of fretfulness, anger and impatience. I have probably sometimes carried a scowl on my face for an hour together. For the most part, however, it was not so. During the greater part of the time, I succeeded in maintaining the signs and manifestations of cheerfulness. One series of failures arose from a source which will be mentioned in the next section.

This is the proper place for mentioning a gross failure, on my part, of teaching as I ought to have done, by my example.

The inhabitants of the district, for the most part, kept Saturday evening, instead of Sunday evening, as a part of the Sabbath. With me, however, it was different. I kept Sunday evening; and my pupils knew it. A few indeed of the people whose children were under my charge, were in this respect, with me.

But whether they kept Sunday evening or Saturday evening, it was customary to meet at a store in the district on Sunday evening, in a kind of club, and read the papers, and discuss politics. Old and young were accustomed to be present; and though there was seldom, if ever, any drinking or profanity, the conversation was often such as ill became those who regarded it as a part of the Lord's day.

And yet, in the face of all this, and of the knowl edge I had of the power and efficacy of example I did not hesitate sometimes, to attend. I tremble when I think of it. But so it was ; and I canno now recall the past. The mischief which I have done, in this way, is done irrevocably.

SECTION X.

MY ILL HEALTH.

Exposure to Cold. Remedies. Opium. Its remote effects. Its happy effects while it lasted. Who ough to be temperate. Who are not.

In consequence of various causes to which had been for many years subjected, I had acquir ed a habit of sometimes suffering severely in th winter from colds. This winter, especially, I wa a great sufferer. I also had slight attacks of rheu matism. The latter however, were far from be ing severe.

For a few years I had used no ardent spirits i any form whatever. Once when I began to fee the effects of taking cold, I used to take a littl spirit, to induce a perspiration ; and as I the supposed, to throw off the disease. Now, instea of spirits, which I was too much of a temperanc man to use, I took for the same purpose, a small pill of opium.

This drug had apparently, a most happy effect on me at all times; but especially when I fancied myself a little ill. While its effects lasted, I was all cheerfulness and health and happiness. All seemed to go well, too, in the school room. In short, so happy were its immediate results, that I became almost a slave to its use; and I wonder, now, why I did not become quite so.

For so frequent were my colds, and rheumatic attacks, and so frequently were they feared, as coming on, and so numerous were my other ailments, that sometimes scarcely a day in a week passed in which I did not resort more or less to the opium. The quantity I took at each time was indeed very small; but it had the desired effect. It threw me into a gentle perspiration, tranquillized and even cheered my mind, made me strong in body, gave me courage, and did almost everything to tempt me to resort to it again the very next time I was inclined to do so.

How strange that I did not perceive that many of the miserable feelings which I experienced, at times,(and which joined with other causes in tempting and seducing me,) were caused by the very opium itself which I had before taken! That is to say, the opium had left my nervous system in

such an irritable state as to expose me to suffer
ing from causes which, had I let opium alone, nev
er would have given me much trouble.

While the effects of the opium lasted however
as I have already intimated, I was a very happy
man, and an excellent school-master ; yes, and
had most excellent pupils. You cannot think how
finely they behaved and recited, and what wonder
ful progress they made—in my own imagination a
least—while I was under the influence and ex
citement of the narcotic drug.

But when the effects of this base deceiver wer
gone, how was everything changed! How
roguish, how ungovernable, were the scholars
How little they cared for books or learning
How gloomy everything appeared, how dismal my
prospects! How pale my countenance, and how
unfavorably it affected the feelings, and ultimately
—as I imagined—the conduct of the pupils !

If there be a man on earth who ought to le
alone everything calculated to produce nervou
excitement, it is the school master. If there be a
person who ought to let alone not only all distill
ed and fermented liquors, but all narcotic drinks
drugs, medicines, etc., it is the school master. I
there be a person on earth who ought to show him
self a pattern of temperance in all things, and
avoid in every respect, all infringement of the

aws of the human frame, it is the school mas-
er.

And yet there are school masters—some few—
vho still drink cider, beer, wine, tea, coffee, etc.
There are those who smoke cigars, and perhaps
hew tobacco. There are those who eat—if
hey can get it—highly exciting food. In short,
ngaged as they are, in a very exhausting em-
loyment, and feeling or imagining they feel the
eed of some physical excitement or other, there
re not a few of them who resort, in an unguard-
d hour, to something which may be as hurtful,
erhaps in the end, as an occasional pill of opium.

Let all such teachers beware. Let them re-
nember their high responsibility. If they lived
olely to and for themselves, the case would be
omewhat altered. But their faults, as seen
hrough their example, may affect, sooner or later,
he character of hundreds, if not of thousands.

SECTION XI.

COUNTENANCING THE SPORTS OF MY PUPILS.

Should teachers join in the sports of their pupils? Reasons in favor of the practice. Ball playing. Coasting. Skating. Remarks on skating and playing on the ice. Going out in the evening. If done, parents or teachers should oversee. Dancing—its general use. An anecdote. Another error. Effects. Reflections.

It was not common for teachers, in the vicinity of the district where I now resided, to engage in the sports of the pupils. My immediate predecessor, however, had done it. There was a very general prejudice against it, but he had dared to oppose it; and I found the majority of the people, after all, in its favor.

This was all very well; and I was glad to see such an unreasonable prejudice giving way. was and still am a full believer in the propriety and even necessity of the teacher's mingling in the sports of his pupils. And although I have already adverted to the subject once or twice briefly, I must be indulged in a few more remarks on the same subject.

1. The sports of pupils are excellent for studying their disposition and character. In the school

25*

ᴐom they may be more or less disguized ; but in ᴉeir sports, they are sometimes, incautiously, off ᴉeir guard ; and they then show themselves out ᴉ their true naked character.

2. To join them, in their sports, is an excellent ᴉeans of controlling the character and regulating ll the circumstances of their recreations, in such way as to render them salutary ; and not only ᴉ physically, but morally.   This whole subject— ᴇ healthfulness of children's sports especially— greatly overlooked.

3. The practice will have a favorable influence ᴉ the health of the teacher himself.   He needs ᴄercise in the open air, as well as his pupils. ᴇ might indeed walk or work ; but in that case ᴐugh his body would be exercised, his mind ᴐuld not always be relieved ; and this portion of ᴇ human being, immured as it is, quite too long, the school house, needs recreation quite as much the body does.

But besides the immediate effects of free exer- ᴣe in the open air, it greatly favors his health ᴐre remotely.   It preserves, in some measure, ᴉt only his bodily elasticity, but the elasticity of ᴣ mind.   It revives and preserves juvenile feel- ᴣs, habits, and manners.   In a word, there is one thing more useful, in every point of view, the country school master—and the school master in the town or city needs it still more—than frequent free exercise out of doors with his pupils.

Our most common exercise was ball playing. In this, I was not very expert; but I believe I had all the healthful advantages which pertain to it, notwithstanding. It is really an excellent sport. I wish none of the sports of the young were more doubtful, in their tendency.

Another favorite amusement was coasting. In this, however, we found difficulties. Situated as the roads were, in our vicinity, we should have been compelled to go into the fields to amuse ourselves in any considerable degree with coasting. But this the owners of the fields were unwilling we should do. For this prohibition, there were various reasons; some of them reasons of weight.

Another amusement was skating and playing on the ice. The only objection to this was that the " pond," to which we were accustomed to resort, was rather too far from the school house. To go there during the short recess, at the middle of the forenoon and afternoon, was impossible. And as a large proportion of us went home for our dinners, it was almost impossible to find any time during the regular intermission. The distance was about three quarters of a mile; we had therefore, barely time to spare from our dinners run to the pond, and then run back again; without staying to play a moment. But this would not do. The temptation to stay a little while was so great; and as boys seldom think, in such cases, how rapidly time flies, there was a strong probability their stay would interfere with the hours of school.

The only time, therefore, which was left us for this exercise was the evening; and to the evening it was chiefly confined. I do not remember that I had much trouble from their going on the pond at noon; on the contrary, I well remember that the far greater part of them were sure to be at the school room by one o'clock. My own example of punctuality had been effectual this winter, as well as on a former occasion.

There are many objections to the practice of going out to skate or coast in the evening, especially to skate on the ice; and some of them are very serious and weighty. One is that children ought to be at home, in the evening, in the bosom of the family. Another is, that if they go out they are apt to stay so long, that they get to bed later than usual. Another is, that all the purposes of health are better subserved by their staying within doors. Another still, is, that if there should be holes or dangerous places in the ice, they are not so well seen in the night as in the day time.

If, however, in spite of these objections, boys are suffered to go abroad in the evening for the purposes here mentioned, some judicious father or teacher, ought always to accompany them Thus they would endeavor to guard them from danger to soul as well as to body ; and they would remind them of the hour when it was proper for them to return.

In this sport, of skating in the evening, I never joined my pupils. I only prohibited the exercise during the hours when the pupils were under my more immediate direction, leaving it to the parents to give them permission to go out in the evening or not, according as they thought proper.

One great advantage would have been derived from my going out with them more than I did even though it were in the evening. The young seem to think their parents and teachers grudge them time for sport, and would gladly cheat them out of it entirely, if they could. Now I must own that there are many parents and some teachers who do so ; and therefore the opinion is not wholly unfounded. But whether well founded or not it exerts an unhappy influence. It leads children to estimate recreation higher than they ought, and higher than, in other circumstances, they would be apt to estimate it.

But this error might be, in a good measure pre

vented, if parents and teachers would indulge those under their care with a pretty full measure of time for recreation, and let them see, by their whole conduct, that they do it cheerfully and not grudgingly ; and if, above all, they would occasionally make one of the party, and join them heart and hand, in everything but that which is morally wrong.

One circumstance connected with this subject of recreation deserves to be mentioned, as it is, I think, quite instructive.

I had not only an eye to the sports of the male pupils, but also to those of the females. These last were usually within doors ; and for this purpose, I used always to give up, during the intermission, my schoolroom ; sometimes when it was quite a self denial, not to say a sacrifice. Exercise, I knew they must have ; and there was no other good way for them to secure it, in bad or winter weather, than by recreation within doors.

There were in the school a number of young ladies twelve, fourteen, or sixteen years of age. Some of them were already in a bad state of health, and I feared that being confined to the seats of the school room six hours a day, without something to counteract the dangerous tendency of so doing, would make their condition still worse.

For persons who sit much, such as students,

shoemakers and tailors, I had long been of opinion that dancing was a most salutary exercise ; and had not hesitated on all proper occasions to say so. I had done it too, in the face of the opinions of one or two sects of Christians, who in view of the evils which are too often associated with this exercise, go the length of denouncing it altogether

One day, having been absent a short time from my school room, during the hours of play, I returned, unexpectedly, and found the girls dancing So far was I from discouraging the practice, that I gave it my entire approbation ; and even recommended the continuance of it. In doing this, I had reference, principally, to the health of those who were already feeble. Had every pupil enjoyed perfect health, I do not think I should have said anything about it, either to approve or disapprove.

It happened that one of the families which lived near the door of the school house belonged to one of those sects of Christians who are greatly opposed to dancing. This family, as I have every reason for believing, felt very much hurt, by having singing and dancing, every day at noon, so near them ; and above all, to learn that it was countenanced and encouraged by the teacher.

Of this, however, I thought nothing at all, at the time. The tendency of the mistake—for I think does not deserve a smoother name—was only iscovered, some time afterward, in a case which ill be mentioned in our next section.

The purposes which were contemplated in ranting permission to dance, were, I fully believe, ccomplished. I have no doubt it was a salutary heck to the deleterious tendency of the school ench and school atmosphere. Every one seemed nvigorated and made happier by it, except one, ho was so far gone with consumption that she ever became very vigorous; though even she ppeared to receive temporary benefit.

My error in this consisted, in not taking into onsideration public sentiment. I well knew the eligious scruples of the neighbors, and ought herefore to have avoided offending them. Or if had done no more, a plain statement of the vhole case, with my reasons for every step I had aken, with expressions of regret that I found it lecessary to their health, would perhaps have been idvisable.*

This, however, was not my way of doing things. was accustomed to do what I thought at the time

---

* There are, however, objections to dancing, founded n the constitutions of the young, at the period of life f which I am now speaking, which are usually over-ooked; but which I have not room—were this work the lace for it—fully to discuss.

to be right, without much regard to consequences Sometimes the results satisfied me ; sometime they did not.——It is a pity we cannot combine witl a strong determination to do what is right, the ha bit of taking consequences into the account ; a these often have their use, in enabling us to de termine what right is.

There was one circumstance connected witl the dancing, which I forgot to mention. The gen tleman, whose family feeling I have mentioned had laborers—young men—in his employ, eithe as apprentices or journeymen ; for I have forgot ten which. These young men used sometime to steal away and go to the school room to join ii the dancing. Not often, it is true, but yet ofter enough to excite the displeasure, and rivet the prejudices of their employer.

SECTION XII.

DISCIPLINE.

General success. Case of obstinacy. My views, at
that time, of corporal punishment. Infliction of punishment. An angry father. His treatment of me.
Reflections. Explanation of the matter. Taking part
with the father. Discussion of the subject with a
friend. His narrow views of punishment. Why I
took no pains to see the father. Consideration of the
subject. Over tenderness. An anecdote. A caution.
Proportion of the punishment to the crime. Mistakes
of parents and teachers. Marks on the skin. Observations on punishment.

In the discipline and general management of
my school, I succeeded better this winter, than on
any former occasion, with the exception of perhaps one or two instances. I had indeed frowned,
and sometimes complained; especially when under the influence of opium. But I had succeeded
without much severity of any kind; and had rid
myself entirely of the wretched habit of boxing the
ears and striking the head. I was now resolved,
if I punished at all, to do it on philosophical principles; to do it for the child's good; and to do it
in such a manner, and with such a spirit, as would
not cause subsequent regret.

Nearly the whole term had passed away, and

nothing had occurred to give uneasiness in the district, so far as I then knew; for the effects which the dancing had produced on some few minds had, thus far been concealed from me. Nor do I recollect that I had used a rod or ferule, in more than one or two instances, during the whole winter.

But I had one small pupil who, for some reason or other which I could not then discover, became quite disobedient. He had an elder brother in school a part of the time. The elder boy was famous for slyness, and though I had reason to think he did some things which were not according to rule, I could not so easily detect him. But the little boy—now about seven or eight years old—was more open in his conduct, and more easily detected.

He was often caught in his roguish tricks, and often admonished. At last his conduct appeared to assume the character of obstinacy, and I began to think it necessary to threaten. This, at first, made a slight impression, but soon wore out. From threats, I resolved at length to proceed farther, and to put my threats of punishment into execution.

My opinion, at this time was, that neither the rod nor indeed corporal punishment of any kind should be used on children from two to ten years of age, except in case of obstinacy; and that whenever it was used, its use should be persevered in till the child was made to yield. To stop before we gained our point, and induced submission, was in ordinary cases, to spoil the child. I had arrived at this conclusion, both from experience and much observation. It is also confirmed in the writings of Locke, Witherspoon, and others.

The particular act of misconduct of which the boy whose case I am going to relate was guilty at the time when I inflicted punishment, was not, in itself considered, a crime of magnitude. It was only great by its relations. It was one of a series of transgressions, or rather defiances of law, which he had long been perpetrating with the constant and steady assurance that a penalty would follow, unless he desisted. But he did not desist, and the penalty was inflicted.

The infliction was simply a chastisement with a rod of appropriate size. This, I say, was the simple fact. But there were, connected with it, many little circumstances which gave it the appearance of more than ordinary severity. One of these was requiring him to take off his coat. Another was a good deal of preparation and parade; as if something terrible was to be done. Another, still, was the long continuance of the punishment. I struck a few blows, then paused, and conversed with him ; then repeated the blows, and so on. All this was designed as a means of accomplishing, in the most effectual manner, the desired result—the correction of the transgression, and the prevention of its recurrence.

The punishment was inflicted at the close of the afternoon. When it was over, I thought no more of it. The consciousness that I had done my duty, disagreeable as it was, and the hope that it would accomplish the objects intended, were so strong that I do not recollect ever thinking of the possibility that any individual would be dissatisfied.

But early the next morning, as I was making my fire at the school room as usual, in came the boy's father, and immediately began to complain of me for abusing his child. He was evidently in anger ; I therefore said as little as I could to him, and at the same time give him reason to understand I had only done my duty.

But my comparative coolness and candor seemed to enrage, rather than quiet him. He accused me of cruelty and tyranny, in whipping, unmercifully, a poor motherless boy ; and that too, for just nothing at all. He said he had heretofore thought very well of me, but that he now regarded me as a monster ; and that the people of the district were of the same general sentiment with himself.

In the course of his conversation he alluded to

certain marks which he said were made on the boy's back by the whip, and which were visible for many hours after he got home from school. In short, he gave full vent to his feelings, and then left me.

I am always pleased with the plan of going directly to the teacher and making complaints to him, before we publish what we conceive to be his errors, to the world. In this instance, however, as I afterwards learned, the father had reported the story, with much exaggeration of circumstances, in several other places; and had succeeded in enlisting against me the prejudices of several other persons, especially a very aged lady, and one man a very whimsical opium taker. I also found—to my great surprise, at first—that the persons who were displeased, with the exception of the two I have just named, were brethren of the same denomination of Christians; and were the very persons who had been offended, by the dancing!

Could there have been a doubt in my mind, reader, why the father of the boy whom I had punished made such an unreasonable ado? Will any one believe it would have been so, had there been no offence given by the dancing?

He charged me with imbecility, insanity, and everything else. His charges were even so ex-

travagant that had it not been known he was of
a most impetuous temper, he would have defeated
his own purpose—that of enlisting sympathy—by
his very violence.

And yet this man was a professor of religion—
the christian religion—the religion of Jesus ! But
I will not be thought disposed to recriminate. He
has gone to render his final account !

Among those who took his part was a neighbor
of his, a former acquaintance and distant relative
of my own. He found fault with me, because I
punished the boy for a mere trifle. I asked him
if he knew what it was for which I punished him.
He said the children stated it so and so—naming
some little tricks, such as children are wont to
play. I told him he was not punished for any one
act, independent of all other acts ; but for obstinacy in persisting to do what I had forbidden him ;
that the particular act which took place at the
time, was only one of a series of transgressions
prompted by obstinacy, which had been running
on for some time.

But either he could not or would not understand
this, and still persisted in his charge that the punishment was disproportioned to the crime. Why,
said he, there were marks on the boy's skin for
twenty-four hours afterward. Was the skin broken ? I asked. Oh no, but there were red streaks.

Can you punish an obstinate boy, of his age, with the rod, I asked, to any purpose, without marking his skin ?

This, he said, he could not tell ; for he had never punished so small a boy with severity. Little boys, he said, should be whipped often and but little at a time. Large punishments might do for larger boys, but not for small ones.

It is of little use to discuss the principles of punishment with persons whose minds are so contracted as was the mind of this young man ; but I could not resist the temptation to make a few statements on the subject. To silence, by our arguments, is by no means to convince ; and I was, in the end, obliged to leave him, as far from just views on the subject as I had found him.

So conscious was I of having done right in the case, that I neglected to call and see and examine the boy, which I now very much regret. He came to school as usual, it is true, but I did not like to examine his back at the school room.

Had the father been either a sensible or a reasonable man, I would have gone to his house, and talked the matter over with him. But he was one of those who will not yield a point, even if convinced of being in the wrong. That is to say, he was one of the ignorant ; for to resolve not to see thing in a different manner from what we now see it, is one of the surest known marks of a contracted mind, which the world can afford.

Had I met with him and talked the matter over, I doubt whether anything would have been gained. He was fixed in his own way and belief, and it is not likely that anything I could have said would have convinced him of the reasonableness of my conduct. He would still have believed, in all probability, that *little* children—especially *motherless* children, must be punished " little and often ;" that the punishment was disproportioned to the error ; and that the marks on the poor boy's skin were certain signs of an unreasonable degree of violence, and of cruelty and tyranny.

But though we never discussed the subject, together ; and though it is now too late to discuss it for his benefit, it may be useful to others to consider for a few moments these charges, thus preferred against me ; for they were not peculiar to this case ; many a better man than myself has found them preferred against him.

The little boy, it was represented, was motherless ; by which in the present case, was only meant that he had lost his *own* mother. She died several years before. But her place was very nearly supplied by an excellent step mother. This, therefore, were it a valid reason for increased tenderness in any case, was no reason at all for any variation of treatment by me.

Nor is misfortune of any kind whatever, a sufficient reason for that 'increased tenderness which better deserves the name of indulgence. On this rock, multitudes have split. A most fatal mistake! And if this work should save from perdition a few of these poor children who would otherwise be destroyed—in soul if not in body—by its influence, I should think myself amply repaid for the task of presenting it to the public.

I know, very well, how common it is to injure children, by this undue—this misplaced tenderness. The child is fatherless or motherless; or —poor thing!—it has lost an eye, or is without hearing, or speech; or it is deformed! It must not, therefore,—all unfortunate as it is—be corrected for its faults; certainly with any severity; —Oh no; it would be cruel. Thus many people reason on the subject, if reason it may be called.

A certain lady had a younger daughter, who was a little deformed, in several respects. Her eldest daughter had been well brought up; but this unfortunate one must be indulged. The mother could not bear to chide her; above all to whip her. Or if she struck her at all, it was in a fit of passion—across the head, perhaps—for which she reproached herself five minutes afterwards; and to atone for which she gave her poor injured abused darling a piece of sugar or a kiss.

But such a state of things could not last. The child's temper gradually became so ungovernable that if the mother did not actually resort to the rod, as an instrument of correction, she punished her a thousand times worse, by her frowns, and by frequently scolding at her. Nor was this by any means the worst of the evil. The daughter, herself, is the great sufferer. She finds herself—for she is a woman of thought—doomed to the society of a temper which costs her daily and hourly a tremendous amount of suffering. And though I believe she will, in the end, partly overcome it by the force of christian principle, it had been much better never to have formed it. Here is cruelty with a vengeance. To bring suffering, like this, on our children, and thus punish them all the days of their lives for our own negligence or error is something at which every feeling heart should shudder. Yet this is the wisdom of many. It was the wisdom of the father above mentioned, and some of his neighbors.

Here let parents and teachers—should this meet their eye—pause a moment, and consider their ways! Let them consider whether they may not be bringing wo upon their offspring in this very way. Let them see whether their own sins, in this respect, are not likely to be visited upon their children, unto the third and fourth generation!

n regard to the objection of the father of the
le boy, or rather of his neighbor, my young
nd, for him, that the punishment was dispro-
tioned to the crime, I have perhaps, said all
t is necessary. I will add however, that if my
ws on this subject, viz. that corporal punishment
uld, for the most part, be inflicted—not indeed
h clubs, but—with a small rod ; if it should
dom or never be inflicted except for any long
tinued obstinacy ; and if, when the child is ac-
lly corrected, it should be just sufficient to over-
ne that obstinacy, and no more without much
perhaps without any—reference to that particu-
act in the series of acts by which the obstina-
was manifested upon whose recurrence, the
nishment was inflicted ;—if these views, I say,
just, then a pretty large proportion of parents
l teachers are in the wrong, in their daily prac-
.

Children are oftener punished in proportion to
inconvenience their conduct has produced at
moment, to the parent or teacher who punishes,
n with a reference to their own good, present
l future. I will not exempt from this charge
ne very wise and good persons—wise and good,
nean, in the general acceptation of the terms.
ildren are oftener, I repeat it—made to suffer,
the present and in the future, for the sins and

follies of those who are set over them, than for their own voluntary misconduct.

Such was peculiarly the case with the boy, whose story has given rise to these remarks and reflections—and I say again; why in the name of mercy herself, will not parents and teachers consider? Why will they not take time to look into this subject?

I will tell you why. Their whole souls, as a too frequent rule, are absorbed in efforts to get money. The great object is, not to form the minds and hearts of their children—to train them for their country and for God—but to heap up property for them, or at least to *preserve*, both for themselves and their children, the semblance of wealth to-day, come of the morrow what may.

This father was a man of much property, and he had earned it by unwearied exertion, at home and abroad. For years he had absented himself from the bosom of that family who needed, daily, the instruction and assistance of the father whom God had set over them, in order to gain money. And he succeeded; he accomplished his object; but oh, at what a tremendous expense! Nay, what was the gain to himself, personally, to say nothing of the neglected moral character of his family?

But to the remaining charge against me, that

27

ere were marks on the boy's skin for some twen-
-four hours after the punishment. Now it is not
uite *certain* that any marks really existed, but I
iink it quite probable.   I think nothing is more
atural than that streaks on the skin should have
een, for a short time, perceptible.   But suppose
ll this is conceded, what then ?   Does it prove
iat there was abuse ?   Does it at all indicate an
nreasonable degree of severity ?

I do not hesitate to maintain—and with much
onfidence—that it is not easy to inflict punish-
ient with the rod, in a degree which would be cal-
:d but reasonable severity, without leaving on the
cin, the marks of the instrument.   But these
iarks do no harm ; none at all.   They pass
way, in a short time.   Even if there were to re-
iain—for a week or more—a purplish appearance,
idicating that the skin is slightly bruised, it could
ot possibly affect the general health of the child.

Are we to stop short of a point in our correc-
on, which alone will secure its end, for fear of
ijuring the skin a little ?   Are we to jeopardize
ie child's soul for fear marks should remain, a
ay or two, on his skin—a part so unessential to
fe ?   It is painful to me to dwell on this topic,
ecause I feel morally certain that all this punish-
ient of the body, for the past, might be prevent-
d.   But, though painful, it must be dwelt upon,

till the subject is understood. And I do not hesitate to repeat, what I have practically said before, that as the world now is, it cannot safely be foreborne. There are errors, in most children, which must be corrected, or they must experience future suffering in a degree, with which the pain of any common or parental or pedagogical punishment can bear no comparison. Now if there is good reason to hope we can prevent the greater *future* suffering, by the small suffering of the *present*, is it not proper that the latter should be inflicted ?

The least measure of pain, however, which will answer the purpose, should of course be applied; whether it be pain of mind or body. Whether the application shall be to the mind or the body, or to both, is to me, a matter of less consequence; though I prefer to inflict it on the body. I have none of that modern fastidiousness about *whipping*, as it is opprobriously called, which would lead me to inflict an unreasonable degree of mental suffering on my child, simply to avoid it.

Many of these very parents who would not for the world, use the rod on a child ! lest they should permanently injure or degrade him, or diminish his self respect, will not hesitate to box his ears, strike his head with a book, or his body with a rule, a hoe handle or a broom. And yet are not these forms of punishment equally degrading with the use of a rod of suitable size, and much more injurious? But I have dwelt on this painful topic, at sufficient length elsewhere. I will only say that the father, above mentioned, was not only accustomed to beat and bruise the bodies of his children in a very unreasonable manner, but also to keep them almost constantly miserable in their feelings, whenever he was present.

May this section, and the facts and considerations and reflections it contains, have their intended effect! May they lead parents and teachers to pause, reflect and beware! Could we estimate properly, the height, the depth, the length and the breadth of human responsibility, how would it—at least, how ought it to affect our conduct! Whether we sustain the relation of parent, guardian, master, or teacher, we are giving shape to character for time and eternity. In the family, in the school, everywhere—by our lessons, our instructions of every sort, our example in everything—we are forming mind and heart for the great future, and preparing the immortal spirit, with which we have to do, for inconceivable joy, or an inconceivable amount of suffering.

END.

CPSIA information can be obtained
at www.ICGtesting.com
Printed in the USA
BVHW041443140819
555860BV00026B/2240/P